BE A HUMBLE WINNER

BE A HUMBLE WINNER

Suresh Mohan Semwal

Ocean Books Pvt. Ltd.

ISO 9001:2015 Publishers

Published by
Ocean Books (P) Ltd.
4/19 Asaf Ali Road,
New Delhi-110 002 (INDIA)
Phs. : 011-23289555 • 23289666 • 23289777
E-mail: info@oceanbooks.in

ISBN 978-81-8430-401-5
BE A HUMBLE WINNER
by Suresh Mohan Semwal

Edition
2020

Price
₹ 150.00 (Rupees One Hundred Fifty only)

Printed at
Narul Printers, Delhi

~~~~~~~~~~~~~~~~~~~~~~~~~~~~~~~~~~~~

I dedicate my first book to my mother,
Mrs. Kamaleshwar Semwal, from whom
I have received the inspiration to fulfil my
Responsibilities with Selflessness and
Smiling with love.

~~~~~~~~~~~~~~~~~~~~~~~~~~~~~~~~~~~~

Be A Humble Winner

One mistake we continued making throughout our lives; the dust was actually on our faces but we continued cleaning the mirror.

If I were to ask you to pen down the top ten reasons for your success in life. What would you write? I know you can't just write ten, there will be thirty reasons. But still in your top 10 list you might have the following reasons:

1. Hardwork
2. Commitment
3. Patience
4. Honesty
5. Discipline
6. Dedication
7. Positive Attitude
8. Skills
9. Education
10. Attention to details

All the above must be true, no doubts about that. But have we forgotten something? One is too small a number to achieve significant success. One can only start but can't finish without other's support. Sometimes successful people start believing in the statement that "I am a self-made person." I find this statement to be highly ignorant or arrogant. None of us can be self-made. We always had, we all do and will always require other's support to achieve significant success.

We have a very natural tendency to overestimate our contribution in case of success and underestimate in case of failure. Is it not so? There are always people who help/assist/guide/supervise/motivate us to attain success. We tend to remember those who hurt rather than who help. If we really observe our life events and success we will realise that there are many people without whom we could not have become successful.

I recently came across a beautiful story and would like to share here with you. This story will help us to understand it aptly.

"Who is packing your parachute?"

Air Commodore Vishal was a Jet pilot. In a combat mission his fighter plane was destroyed by a missile, He however ejected himself and parachuted safely. He won acclaims and appreciations from many. After five years one day he was sitting with his wife in a restaurant. A man from another table came to him and said, "You are Captain Vishal. You flew jet fighters. You were shot down!"

"How in the world did you know that?" asked Vishal.

"I packed your parachute", the man smiled and went away. Vishal gasped in surprise and gratitude. He realized that if parachute hadn't worked, he wouldn't be here today. Vishal could not sleep that night, thinking about that man. He wondered how many times I might have seen him and not even said 'Good morning, how are you?' or anything because he was a fighter pilot and that person was just a safety worker."

So friends, who is packing your parachute? Everyone has someone who provides what they need to make it through the day. While we as winners are busy celebrating our success we must not forget those who have been silently working hard without making any fuss about it to ensure that we remain winners. Therefore, every winner must be humble and thankful to all those who are directly or indirectly responsible to make us what we are today as winners.

"Humility prevents humiliation."

We have been always encouraged to be winners all the time in everything. Ever since we take our first steps we are taught that all that matters is winning. What we don't realize is that it is equally important that our winning should not create losers around us. No man is an island, we can't achieve success in isolation. There are many variables that contribute into making a successful winner.

Then why the arrogance of assuming 'I' achieved success. I am number one. I am a winner. Humility is acknowledging that we can't achieve anything alone. A rose can blossom only with the right soil, water and sunlight. It also needs some protector too. Even then it needs the breeze to carry it's fragrance.

An attitude of gratitude creates good feeling around us and makes everyone who has contributed in the success story to feel like a winner. Real winners lift others as well. So, be a winner but ensure that you remain humble. Laugh with people not at people. Always acknowledge, appreciate and remember what all good others have done for us. Be a humble winner!

—Suresh Mohan Semwal

I have used many incidents and stories in this book. Incidents which I have read or heard somewhere in my life and the credit for which goes to their respective authors.

Contents

"Only if you take on the responsibility of your condition and the circumstances will you be able to improve upon them."

1

Responsibility...A Feeling

Responsibility is such a word that the moment you hear it, you get a mixed feeling. While some consider it a burden, others consider it the purpose of life. Some consider responsibility as their work and duty. The question here is not what one considers it but what is the effect of adopting different attitudes or outlooks for only that one thing.

Burden or purpose of living—Responsibility is associated with every work. If we say that it is useless to hope for success in any work, without fulfilling our responsibility in a proper manner, then it will not be wrong. If we consider a responsibility is our own and fulfil it, then we can achieve self-satisfaction, joy and happiness, and if we are compelled to fulfil our responsibility, then we will get the feeling of having somehow, completed the work. Now this thing is worth self-contemplation whether the work should be done with responsibility or by considering it a burden and how you want to feel after finishing the work.

I do not want to exert my opinion on anyone in this connection, but according to the experience that I have gained during the seminars in this short life of mine, I have seen that when a person takes on any responsibility according to his own desire, then that becomes his strength and becomes the purpose of living his life, but when the same responsibility has to be taken under compulsion, then it gives us the feeling of being a burden. Only 20% of the responsibility can be given but 80% has to be taken. Hence, responsibility is not given, it is taken.

However, the question here is not of 'has to be taken' or 'want to take'; it is of the feeling of responsibility. In order to explain what I am trying to say, I shall present before you an incident from one seminar of mine. I had gone to Lucknow to arrange for a seminar. I was to address some managers there. I have habit of asking too many questions. It is my belief that there is no dearth of knowledge amongst us; the only thing we lack is thinking in the right direction and acting on the knowledge. Hence, by asking questions during a seminar, I only encourage my participants to think.

Why are You Living?

In that seminar, I asked the question, "Why are you living?" The moment this question was asked, everyone started looking at each other with amazement, but no one gave any reply. I can't tolerate laziness or lazy people in a seminar. Lazy people seem like corpses to me and however dear the corpses might be, no one likes to keep it with himself for very long.

One gentleman was sprawled on his chair in extreme laziness (some people have this kind of a habit). I did not like his way of sitting. Leaving everyone, I went to him and asked him, "Sir, can you tell me why you are living?" He found this question rather awkward. He felt a little bad also about why, leaving everyone aside, I had gone to him only to ask such a silly question! He may probably have thought if amongst all the people only he was living? He paid no heed to that what I had said and started turning the folders before him, so that I may go to someone else, but I, with determination, continued standing beside him and, once again, said to him, "Sir, you may see this folder comfortably after 5 o'clock. For the present, can you please give an answer to my question?" When I continued standing there for quite some time, he turned towards me and smiled and thought that may be, he would be able to get rid of me but he was not aware of why I was asking him that question. With determination, I continued standing before him and repeating my question. Anger had now replaced the smile. He suddenly got up and banging his hands loudly on the table, said, "What else shall I do? Die? What kind of a question is this? Why are you living? My dear brother, what can I do. Get up in the morning, my eyes opened. I was alive, so I came. Had my eyes not opened, I would have continued lying there." Then, as if trying to throw the ball into my court, he said to me, "Alright, you only tell me why we are living? And why did you ask this question to me only?" With agitation, his entire laziness had gone away. Now, with the hope of collecting the support of all other participants, he sat straight in his chair. Now, I really liked his sitting straight on the chair. I said, "Sir, if you did not like my question or the way I had asked it, please accept my apologies. I had asked you this question because I felt that for the last 40-50 years, you had just been adding glamour to the earth, so probably, you would know the answer of this question. If you do not know the answer of this question of mine, there is no problem. Please excuse me. It was my fault."

Don't you think that the majority of us would give the same reply of "So what do I do? Die?" Actually, someone had asked me the same question at a seminar but, despite my asking him, he did not give me any answer to this question. What he said was, "How can I tell you why you are living? You will have to search the reason for this yourself." I felt a little peculiar when I heard his reply and if I give the same reply to you people, you will also experience the same disappointment that I had felt. Hence, after doing a lot of research on this topic, I have come to this conclusion. You may disagree with my opinion, but it is my belief that we are alive because we have not died but we are living because we have the responsibility on our heads of keeping six customers satisfied and happy and the same power (not burden) of those responsibilities continues to inspire us, not compels us, to live. And these six customers, towards whom we have a responsibility, are as follows:

1. Self	—	Our first responsibility is towards ourselves
2. Family	—	Personal customer
3. Those who work with us and the Institution	—	Personalised customer
4. Customer	—	Outsider customer
5. Society/Country	—	Social customer
6. God	—	Intimate customer

Self—It is our foremost and most important responsibility. Keeping ourselves physically and mentally healthy is not just our responsibility but also a necessity. Remember, if we are not happy then somewhere, we are ourselves responsible for this. If we feel that the responsibility for our happiness rests with our family, our co-workers or the government, then our being happy will be a little difficult.

Family—We can call the family our personal customers because to keep it happy is our sole responsibility. The only reason why we use the word customer is that we may feel the necessity to keep them happy because we still remember to keep the customer happy but not the family. To make ourselves happy, it is essential to keep the family happy. You must be aware that if the wife is not happy then it becomes very difficult for the husband to remain happy for long. Therefore, if you want to be happy yourself, then you must definitely take care to keep the family happy. In every family, there is one member who never complains, who never asks for anything. That member is the 'mother'. She is the only individual who, without asking for anything, takes care of everyone and keeps forgiving each small and big mistake of ours. It is my belief that all other members, either directly or indirectly, somehow manage to attract our attention. The mother is the only member who never demands nor complains and this, probably, is the only reason why sometimes we do not pay as much attention to the mother's happiness as we pay to the others'. It is my belief that a place where the mother is happy will always have prosperity.

Co-workers and Institution—We spend the major portion of our life at our workplace and by habit, carry the tension, excitement and tiredness of the workplace to our homes. Hence, if we want to be happy in life, then it is essential that we maintain good relations with our co-workers so that we can maintain the joy and the excitement at our workplace and carry the same joy to our home too.

Customer (Outside Customer)—These are those people or customers who use our services or products and pay the price for them.

Of all the customers, he is the one customer, without keeping whom happy, it will be very difficult to keep the other customers happy. It is my belief that the money for the expense for our ration, clothes and all other comforts comes from the pockets of these outside customers. Hence, keeping them happy is our greatest responsibility. If those customers stay happy, then our institution will make progress and the progress of the internal customers depends upon the progress of the institution. If we are happy, then we will work well and therefore, progress and only then will we be able to do something for our family and society.

That is why I often tell people that they must always have an idol of the customer in the temple of their hearts and they must continuously find ways and means of keeping that customer happy.

Society/Country—Man is a social animal and all of us enjoy many such comforts which are very essential for living. Although we do not, in any way, contribute in producing or creating them, yet the whole society benefits from it. For example, farmer, doctor, defence, engineer, etc. Hence, it is also our duty to contribute whatever we can; because if we are unable to do so, then there will probably no difference between animals and us.

God—Our responsibility is also towards that God who has blessed us with brains. The faith that He has placed upon human beings, we must utilize it well in order to bring happiness not just to ourselves but to the lives of others too. It is our responsibility to see that after creating us, He feels proud of His creation and that we all make this world such a beautiful place that even God feels keen to come and live on this earth.

In the end, all I want to say is that these six customers are interlinked and interdependent. Overlooking one can influence or affect the entire chain. You may serialize these six customers according to your desire but do not reduce even one or consider any one less than the other.

It is my belief that if an individual is himself very happy, but his family is not, or the people who are working with him are not happy and his neighbours are fed up of him, then, such a man is fit to be admitted into the lunatic asylum. Hence, only if my customers are happy to be with me, will I prove to be successful in my life and my workplace.

What Happens to Man after He Dies?

After the seminar had ended, a gentleman came to me and said, "I want to ask you one question." I said, "Please ask." He said, "What happens to man after he dies?" I waited a while and then, smiling, asked him, "Sir, don't you think you are asking the wrong man this question?" He said, "No I have heard you since morning and I believe that you can surely throw some light on this." I said, "Look here, Sir, first and foremost thank you very much for having listened to me since morning, but what happens to man after he dies, I do not know; because by God's grace I am not dead yet." He smiled a little and then said, "What are you saying? You are probably joking." I became serious and said, "No, Sir, I am absolutely serious and honestly speaking, I do not even know what happens to man after he dies. I honestly believe that you are also very well aware of this reality." But he stuck to his question. I said, "Look here Mister, if you are a Hindu, you will be cremated and if you are a Christian or a Muslim, then you will be buried." He said, "No, No I am not talking about this, I am talking about the soul. What happens to the soul?" I said, "What happens to the soul, this information you will be able to find on the 'Aastha Channel'. I have no experience or information on this." Then, I asked him, "But what happens before a person dies, should we not know that?" "What happens?", he said. I said, "Sir, one has to 'live' before one dies and living means keeping the people around you (customers) happy."

If we are alive and our customers are angry with us, then what is the use of living? I have often seen people looking for a book in the library. The name of the book is *Life After Death*. People are more worried about the life after they are dead. They do not think it important to worry about what is before them, in their hands. If we can keep our first five customers happy, then the sixth, that is God, will definitely be happy with us. However, we are the most worried about the sixth customer. We must understand that we are dependent on Him, not He on us. Therefore, we must give up worrying about God and do our work very faithfully. What I mean to say is that one should not have a belief in God or should stop praying. What I say is that we must show the same perseverance for our work, factory or workplace as we have towards the religious festivals and festivities. If we fulfil our responsibilities with full devotion, determination and enthusiasm, then the day is not far when our country will be at the apex of prosperity and our name will be amongst the leading countries of the world.

Let Things Go as They May

I have a friend whose name is Ram Bharose. As is his name so is his nature. He is fully dependent on

Ram. A few days back he was making a special prayer to God—'Oh God! Please help me get a lottery of a crore.' I sometimes used to suggest to him that if he had to ask for something, why does he not ask for a lottery of a hundred crores. God does not have a scarcity for anything. He does not have to do a duty from 10 to 6 and save the crore rupees to give to you. All He has to do is, say 'Tathastu' or 'Thy will be done'. Then why not ask for a lottery of a hundred crore of rupees, why only one crore? But he was not greedy; that is why he was praying for a lottery of one crore only. He would go to the temple daily, serve God, burn incense but God would not pay heed to his prayers. Two years passed. One night Ram Bharose had a dream that God had come, He put His hand on Ram Bharose's head and patting him, said to his dear disciple, "Ram Bharose, for the last two years, you have been continuously praying to Me for a lottery of one crore. You are My devotee and I also want to give you the lottery, but son, at least buy a lottery ticket. Tell me, can one win a lottery without buying a ticket?"

Similar is the story of another devotee who knew only how to have faith on God, not on his work. He got the fruit of this in the following way.

Nayansukh

On the shores of a river, in a village, there lived a lazy man named Nayansukh, who had a lot of faith in God. Once the Meteorological Department issued an emergency warning that there is a danger of floods in the village. Hence, the villagers are given the warning to go to places of safety as soon as possible.

Taking all their belongings, the villagers started moving towards secure places as soon as possible, but Nayansukh said, "Nobody can kill a person whom God saves." A stranger stopped before Nayansukh's house and offered to take him to a safe place in his car but Nayansukh rejected the offer saying the same old sentence 'Nobody can kill a person whom God saves.'

In a few days water started filling up the village. Nayansukh moved to the first floor of his house. Just then, a youth came there in his boat and offered him help. But Nayansukh said, "This is the time of test. Nobody can kill a person whom God saves." When, despite repeated offers, Nayansukh did not go, the boatman went away. In a short while, the water level went up so high that Nayansukh had to climb up to the terrace of his house. Just then, a search helicopter saw Nayansukh and threw down a rope to help him and pleaded with Nayansukh to climb up. But, once again, Nayansukh rejected this offer of help and repeated the sentence 'Nobody can kill a person whom God saves.' A helicopter also has its limitations. After some time, it also went away. Soon, the water level went up so high that Nayansukh drowned in it and died.

In heaven, he was standing with a swollen face with his back towards God. When God asked him the reason for his anger, Nayansukh said, "I worshipped You throughout my life, had faith on You. So much so that I did not even care for my life and in the end I had to drown and die." God said, "Nayansukh, the first thing I did was announce a warning, which you turned a deaf ear to. Then, I came with a car and also sent a boat but even then you did not listen to me. Finally, I came in a helicopter too but you did not hold on to the rope. Now you only tell me, what could I do?"

What this story means to say is that even if God wants to help us, He does so only in the form of opportunities. Hence, we need to keep our mental switch on, recognize the opportunities that come our way and not miss out on the chance of getting hold of them.

"God also helps only those who help themselves."

Generally, people have this kind of a mentality only. They do not fulfill their share of responsibility and keep pleading with God. They forget that God also helps only those who help themselves. I usually tell people that they must definitely have faith on God but keep their cars locked. They should not leave the responsibility of guarding the car on God. At least do the work which you can do. If our awareness towards our responsibilities increases, then there is no reason why happiness and success should not enter our lives. Actually, the problem comes up when we consider someone else responsible for our condition whereas we do not pay any attention to our own habits. We ourselves, our habits, our choices, our ideologies and ways of our behaviour are responsible for our circumstances, their reasons and results. There can be no improvement in our condition and circumstance by blaming our parents, education, society, government or our fate/destiny.

Three Kinds of People

After a lot of thinking and intense analysis, I have realized that there are three kinds of people in this world. And these are as follows:

1. **Those who put the blame on others:** Such people consider someone else, and not themselves, responsible for every wrong act done to them. Such a person always has some complaint with others. There is always something or the other lacking in every work. For example, some people always taunt their wives when their child gets less marks in the examination by saying, "See, your child has got such less marks in the exams." And if he receives good marks, then with great pride, he swells up his chest and says, "After all, whose son is he! I work so hard for you people. So, how would he not get good marks." Such people are ever ready to take credit for everything, but if anything goes wrong, then they put blame on someone else.
2. **Those who always make excuses:** These type of people always keep some excuse or the other ready for not doing the work. Such people, generally are of 'poor/helpless mentality' and look for opportunities to gather sympathy of others, which I don't think they get. The reply of such people to everything, generally is a 'no' and they will always give you some excuse for saying 'no'—the work either falls in the category of 'impossible', according to them or

they do not consider themselves capable of doing it—either of these can be possible. Such people are never successful or helpful in either setting up or achieving high aims. Sometimes health, sometimes transport, sometimes the cold, sometimes the heat, sometimes the shortage of something, shortage of cooperation and shortage of information are some such reasons which are always used in every sentence of such people. No sentence of theirs can be complete without 'but' or 'however'. Often lazy or unsuccessful people fall prey to the bad habit of making excuses. It is my belief that making excuses is the easiest thing which good-for-nothing people use as a weapon.

For example, if we ask a thief why he stole, then his reply will be because of unemployment or that he needed to buy medicines for his ailing mother. Some people's reply will be in the typical filmy style that he had only two options before him—'stealing' or 'begging' and his conscious would not allow him to beg. This, however, does not mean that stealing is a better option than begging.

Similarly, if a murderer is asked why he committed the murder, then he will also have the same excuse that he could not control his temper. This, however, does not mean that committing a murder becomes a good thing.

Similarly, one who smokes says that his tension reduces when he smokes. He also has the excuse that smoking works as a medicine when he is tense. This does not mean that smoking becomes a good thing. Whether we agree or not, a wrong is a wrong. What is funny is the fact that we are all aware of what is right and what is wrong, then why excuses?

3. **Responsible person:** Such people change themselves according to circumstances and do not miss any opportunity to bring about any improvement in themselves. Such people learn from every incident, and instead of blaming others, work towards finding a better solution to every circumstance.

   People who take on responsibility and fulfill it successfully are successful on every road of their lives.

Why Cry over Spilt Milk?

An old Chinese farmer, with a stick on his shoulder, was walking down the road. A vessel filled with soya bean soup was hanging at one end of the stick.

It struck against something, the vessel fell down and broke into many pieces. The old farmer continued walking ahead without getting perturbed. One man came running up to him and, in an excited voice, said, "Oh! Don't you know that your vessel had fallen down, has been broken and all the soup has spilt on to the road?"

"Yes," said the farmer, "I know it. I heard the sound of it falling down. The vessel has broken. The soup has spilt. What can I do about this now?"

Please Find a Son-in-Law for My Mother

There is an unmarried girl living near our house. Day in and day out, she continues making only one prayer to God. "Oh, God! Please get my mother a good son-in-law." Many people asked her why she did not request God directly to get her married off soon. Her direct reply would be, "No, I am in no hurry, my mother is in a hurry." The God above heard her and her younger sister was married off.

To put it in a gist, do not consider the Lord above to be a fool. Thinking that by making offerings or gifts to Him and bathing in the Ganges, we can pretend before Him or bribe Him to get our work done, is wrong thinking. It is my belief that God above does not see how you behave in a place of worship. Instead, He sees how honest you are towards your work and how honest you are about doing your work? Besides, do you actually understand your responsibilities? How do you perform them? Remember, God showers His blessings upon us only according to our responsibilities and work and how we perform them because God works with us and not for us.

The Sense of Responsibility

There was a fair going on in a village and there was a well which does not have a slab. One man has fallen inside it and was screaming for help. Just then, a Buddhist monk passes by that way. The monk peeps down and sees that the man who has fallen down is his brother. The man is shouting, "Oh monk, please pull me out. I am dying. I do not know how to swim. Hence, I cannot survive for long. How long can I hold on to the brick." The monk says, "What will you do if you come out. There is sorrow everywhere. Those who are outside the well are also inside a big well. And Lord Buddha has said that life is sorrow. Hence, one cannot get rid of sorrow unless one gets freedom from life. What will you do coming out of the well? Try to come out of life." The man screams, "I shall listen to your sermons. First pull me out." But the monk says, "God has said this also that one must not come in the way of anyone's work. If I save you and you commit theft and murder, then even I will be responsible for it. I shall go my way. You are going your way. Our roads do not meet anywhere. I have my own stream of work." And the monk goes ahead.

Just after him, another monk, who believes in Confucius, comes. He peeps down. The dying man says, "Save me." The person who believes in Confucius says, "I shall definitely save you, you do not worry. In his book, Confucius has written that every well must have a slab over it. A well which does not have a slab, a state that has wells without slabs, the ruler of that state is irreligious. You do not worry. We shall start a movement. We shall have a slab placed on every well." The man says, "How can I not worry? By the time slabs are placed on the wells, I shall die." The man who was a follower of Confucius, says, "It is not just your question. It is a question of society, of everyone. I am there for everyone's service. How can I serve each individual separately and if I serve each individual separately, then what will happen to the society? You do not worry. I am going. I shall start a campaign at the fair just now." The man goes to the fair. He stands on a platform and starts making people understand that there should be a slab on every well. One who places a slab on a well does great service. If a well does not have a slab, the ruler of that state is very irreligious.

After him, one man comes to the slab of the well. He peeps down. The man below screams. He pulls out a rope from his bag, ties the rope and throws the other end into the well and pulls that man out.

Responsibility means taking affirmative initiative and creative work done to improve the condition and circumstances and not put the blame on someone else and make excuses to shirk it.

Responsibility...A Strength

A sage was walking on a hilly road. It was scorching hot. The sun seemed to spit fire. Because of the intense heat and the burden of the luggage, the sage was perspiring profusely. The sage had the weight of his books, his clothing and his bedding on his shoulders. He wiped the sweat off his forehead. Because he was tired, he stopped for a while to rest. Just then he saw that a hill maid was also climbing up the same road. She would have been approximately 15 years old. She had a healthy child sitting on her shoulders. The girl was drenched in sweat and was panting. The sage felt pity for her. He placed his hand on the shoulder of the girl and said, "Daughter, you must be feeling a lot of weight?" The girl looked at the sage from top to bottom with surprise and said, "What are you saying Swamiji! You are the one who is carrying the weight, this is my younger brother."

Responsibility is a feeling, which some people have and some do not have. One should not take the responsibility of the past alone but one should take the responsibility of the present and the future too.

How does One Recognize a Responsible Person?

One who does not blame anyone, does not make excuses and shows it by doing something good. It is not necessary that responsibility has anything to do with the status; because some people fulfill all their responsibilities without holding any post and some people, despite being at responsible positions, behave irresponsibly. Responsibility cannot be given only; in fact, one has to take it just as Bhagat Singh, Vivekananda, Subhash Chandra Bose, etc. did. They had taken up the responsibility of getting freedom for the country themselves. It was not given to them.

□

Inspiration can be here only somewhere around you...the only thing required is to search a little for it.

A Smile is the Splendour of the Face
Rigidness is a Sign of a Corpse

2

The Magic of Enthusiasm

Are You Enthusiastic?

In my seminar, I ask a question: "Are you enthusiastic?" Often, the reply of the people is "sometimes, when something new happens in life, then we are enthusiastic otherwise who gets enthusiastic every day. Everyday it is the same house, work, husband-wife, boss, colleagues, work place—every day, it is the same thing. Then how can there be enthusiasm in life?

However, if we wait for something new to happen to bring enthusiasm and joy into our lives, then there cannot be more than 30-40 occasions in one's life to be happy. How many times will a person change jobs, how many times will he get married, how many houses will he build or how many cars will he buy and how many children will he have? Those people who get bored of doing the same thing or getting the same thing done or have got bored, cannot get cheerful in their lives. How will you feel if some surgeon gets bored of doing surgery, a pilot gets bored of flying a plane, Tendulkar gets bored of scoring runs or if husband and wife get bored of each other?

If you want to stay enthusiastic, then you have to give up the habit of getting bored and put your switch on and take pleasure out of the small joys that you get everyday in your life because someone has rightly said, "There are very few occasions in life for big happinesses but there are thousands of occasions for small happinesses." Hence, keep your mental switch on so that we do not miss the small joys just waiting for the big happinesses.

Laugh! that your entire life becomes a laughter. Live life in such a way that your life becomes a big smile. Live in such a way that a smile spreads in the lives of even those people who are around you. Live in such a way that the entire life becomes a row of blossoming flowers.

Has a laughing person ever committed a sin? It is very difficult that a person who laughs could have committed a murder, a laughing person could have abused any one or committed some misconduct or debauchery. It is impossible to have sin in a laughing person and in a moment of laughter. There is only sorrow, dejection, darkness, burden, heaviness, anger, hatred behind all sins. If once we can give birth to a laughing humanity, then immediately, there will be a

90% reduction in sins. Those people who have made this earth sad have filled this earth with sins.

Is a smile such an expensive thing? What do you have to spend for it? There is a saying in English, "It costs nothing to be kind". One does not have to spend anything to live with love. In fact, what is funny is the fact that one gets so much by living with love. It is difficult to keep an account of what one gets free of cost. If a stranger smiles on the road, see how many smiles he gets in return. How the smell of those smiles inspires us from within. How their song starts playing in our lives and how something starts off in our lives.

Don't ask what we should do and how we should be joyous. To be joyous, remember that anywhere and everywhere, wherever you get a chance to laugh, laugh; wherever you can be happy, you must be happy. An individual just needs a direction. If he can procure this, then only those people will be able to achieve the truth about life who travel with happiness and joy towards the truth of life.

You wake up in the morning. Have you ever thought what you have done after getting up? Have you ever thought that after getting up, the first work should be to have a vision of joy and fulfillment towards life! Did you ever, immediately after getting up, thank life and thank God for having got another day. Life once again, again your eyes have opened, once again light from darkness, waking up from sleep!

Has a sense of gratitude ever arisen in your mind? Have you ever folded your hands and thanked the infinite that He has given you, one who does not have any worth, who had slept the previous night, another day to live. One who cannot believe that he did not have any right, who had no worth, who did not have any ability, will get one more day, had got one more day, one more life!

But, no. We have no feelings, no gratitude, no obligation towards life. We get a life and we show our gratitude towards the useless things. If someone comes to me and gifts me a handkerchief worth four paise, then I say "thank you." Throughout our whole life we never get a feeling of gratitude, do not express any happiness, do not get any pleasure.

The Attitude of Gratitude

There was a king. He had an old servant who had been with him throughout his life. He had such love for that old servant that even at night, that old servant used to sleep in his room only and also travel with him. He used to be with him even in the battlefield and also in the palaces. When the king used to visit any emperor, the old man used to go with the king.

One day, both of them went hunting. They lost their way in the jungle. They rested for a while under a tree. There was a fruit hanging from the tree. When the king sat on his horse, he raised his hand and plucked that fruit. He took out his knife and cut a slice of the fruit and, as was his habit, gave a slice to the old man to taste.

The old man said, "Amazing! Never tasted such a fruit! Will you give me one more slice, my lord? He asked for the second, then the third and the king kept on giving. He had such a look of gratitude in his eyes that the king could not stop him. Then, only one slice was left and that was the only fruit on the tree. He started asking the king for that last slice also. The king said, "You are quite mad. Will you not let me taste even one slice?" "No," he started saying. "No, my Lord, it is very delicious. I will not let you taste it." When he started pulling it out of his hands, the king got angry. He said, "This is the limit. You ate the whole fruit, kept talking about such pleasure and such taste, then won't you let me taste one slice?" But the servant had wanted to pull even that last slice out of his hand.

The king said, "No, this is the limit. I gave you so many slices, that was the limit. But I could not guess that you would not leave even one slice for me." But the servant started saying, "No, my lord!" tears welled up in his eyes. He started saying, "No, no. Please give it to me." But the king forcibly put that slice into his mouth. It was bitter poison! He said, "How mad you are. This is complete poison. Why were you eating it?"

The old man had said, "Why should I complain about getting one bitter fruit from the hands from which I got such sweet fruits to eat. No, no, I am not so ungrateful."

We, however, are all so ungrateful only. We have no knowledge of the unlimited shower of happiness that we received throughout our life; and we are filled with remorse or repentance when some little thing goes wrong. This initiative, this way of looking at life is preparing to be sad and unhappy. Man is unhappy because his way of looking at life is wrong. If we are to achieve happiness, then we will have to deepen our thanks for what we are getting. We will have to acknowledge our gratitude for what we have received. If we have the feeling of gratitude, praise, obligation for what we have received, have been receiving, for the immense joy that is being showered upon us 24 hours, we can get excited, feel joyous.

Most Problems are Born Out of the Lack of New Thoughts

Pleasure means cheerfulness, bliss, amazement and happiness. However, until now, what has been taught in the name of religion is sorrow, what has been taught is a weighty seriousness, a kind of worry, anxiety. Leaving aside man, probably no one in the world is sad; nothing is weighty and serious. The whole life is a singing life.

The whole life appears in various poses in the sound of the colours of life. It is only man who is weighed down, sad. This sorrow, this weightiness, this feeling of sorrow, this lament, this locking oneself from within: how did this fear of a flower, a smile, appearing from somewhere, take birth?

There is darkness in one man's house. He can think in two ways—how can darkness be reduced or how can light be increased? If he thinks of how darkness can be reduced, then he will think about reducing the darkness in this direction, how to get rid of darkness, how to fight darkness?

And remember! No one can either fight darkness or defeat it because there is no darkness. If there was any darkness, we could have fought with it, broken it, efface it. The way if we started searching for how to remove darkness, we get stuck at darkness. We will not even think of light. Our mind will automatically centre around darkness only.

He will think, how do I remove darkness? What kind of a sword should I invent, how much strength should I collect so as to be able to throw this darkness out of my house? He will die but darkness will not be removed. He had started thinking directly about effacing darkness. This is wrong because darkness does not have any power—hence nothing can be done on darkness directly. Even if we want we cannot take buckets full of darkness and throw them out. There is only one way to do it and that is to create light. Darkness is the negative aspect of light, which is created by the lack of light.

Darkness does not have any identity except the absence of light. There is only one way to do it and that is to bring light. For this, one will have to expand one's mental frame and keep its switch on.

Darkness and the Sun

Once darkness went to God with a complaint against the Sun and said, "Oh God! Please make the Sun understand. He is making my life miserable. My existence is in danger because of him." God sent a message to the Sun and told him about darkness's complaint. The Sun heard about the complaint and said to God, "I would like to come myself and meet this complainant; because till today, knowingly, I have not done the work of hurting anybody."

"I do not know who this darkness is and how I am hurting him? Call him to Me so that I may apologise to him for hurting him unknowingly." It is said that for ages, God and the Sun waited for darkness but it could not present itself before them.

Just as darkness is the name given to the lack or absence of light, similarly most of the problems of our life are created because of the scarcity of new thoughts. If we put on our mental switch, then we can definitely find the solutions to these problems.

Sometimes, people at my seminars ask how and how many times must we put our mental switches on; because all the time, someone or the other comes and switches it off. At this, what I have to say is that there is need to switch it on many more times than it is switched off. One who falls down and rises again, reaches his destination and one who cannot do this only remains a stone, a hurdle on the way.

□

> ***If there is life, there are dreams, if there are dreams, there are destinations, if there are destinations, there are distances, if there are distances, there are ways. If there are ways, there are difficulties, if there are difficulties, there is courage, if there is courage, there is faith, if there is faith, there is victory. Because a fighter always wins.***
>
> **—Javed Akhtar**

Failure is an opportunity, when you can make yet another start with more understanding.

3

Keep Your Mental Switch On

Acquiring happiness in life is everyone's aim. There is no human being in this world who does not want to touch the peak of success. If successes and achievements are dear then what is the reason for everyone not being able to achieve success and happiness? Despite the fact that although acquiring happiness, satisfaction and success is everyone's target, all are not able to get it. What is most amazing is the fact that most of the people do not lack brains or knowledge. Although they have knowledge, why can they not get a glimpse of it in their lives and in behaviour? What is the reason that despite immense brilliance within, they are unable to reach the summit where they ought to have been? Why is the condition of some of them like the beggar who sat at one place to beg throughout his life and after whose death, wealth worth crores was found from the same place? Why so? The answer to this question I got when suddenly one night, the lights of only our house went off. According to me, the difference in the success is not because of lack of knowledge, but tripping of their 'mental switch' on small things.

You must have also seen when sometimes, the main switch of your residence or office goes off. Whenever it happens, all lights, fans, air conditioners and machines, etc. goes off. Though, all the things remain in their places, look the same too but they do not work. With the switching off of one switch everything stops, nothing works. Similarly, when a tense situation is created in our lives, our mental switch also trips. We start behaving in a strange or unexpected way. For example, you must also have seen that generally after being rebuked by the boss or a customer, people say, "Yaar, my mood has been spoilt" or "My mood is terribly off today." From their words you can make out that their switch has tripped. To such people, my suggestion is that when they come to know that their mood is off, then why don't they do something to make it alright? When the electricity in your house trips, what do you do? Do you take out the fuse of the neighbours' house too? If our shirt gets dirty from somewhere, then, in order to clean our shirt, will we wipe or rub our shirt with someone else's shirt? No, not at all! Then when we are in off mood, instead of setting our mood right, why do we spoil someone else's mood? Is this not true?

This does not mean that it is a bad thing for the switch to trip or that it should not happen. Such people whose switch does not trip with any incident, are found in the lunatic asylum. It is natural for the switch to trip. The switch does trip under tense situations.

However, it should be switched on as soon as possible. This is the basic difference between successful and unsuccessful people. The switch of successful people trips too, but they switch it on quickly and also keep the switch of other people on. Till such time that our switch is on, enthusiasm of our life is maintained, we feel happy and find the people and the world good; but when the switch goes off we find everything around us sad, depressing and full of faults.

Actually, the world remains the same but our outlook changes. If our switch is on then even when the child breaks a glass tumbler, we will not scold him. Instead we will say, "Doesn't matter, son" And on the contrary, if the switch is off, then even if the glass doesn't break, but just falls down, we lose our temper and raise our hand. The poor child cannot understand that when he broke the glass, nothing was said and now, when it has just fallen down, then he received two slaps. Does this mean then that breaking a glass is better?

One has to Run Faster than You, not the Lion

Once an Indian and a foreigner went to the outskirts of a forest for a morning walk. Suddenly, the Indian started tying his shoe laces quickly. Surprised, the foreigner asked him, "What happened? Why are you suddenly tying the shoe laces in such haste?" He did not say anything, just pointed towards the jungle. The foreigner saw that a lion was coming out of the jungle and walking in their direction only. The foreigner also felt scared. Then, picking up some courage, he said to the Indian, "What do you think? By tying your shoe laces, you will be able to run faster than the lion?" Running without stopping, the Indian said, "I don't have to run faster than the lion; only faster than you. The lion will do the rest of the work." This is common sense. It is not necessary to have a degree to use this. Only the 'mental switch' has to be on.

Similarly, by just keeping his mental switch on, how a frog was able to come out of adverse conditions, you will be able to learn from the story given below.

The Story of the Two Frogs

This is the story of not such a long time ago. There were two frogs. They used to live under a tree on the banks of a lake in the jungle. One day, the two of them thought, "We have not seen the outside world. There must be something outside the jungle too. Come, let us go to the world of the human beings and see."

Taking a little something to eat, they both ventured out. Hopping, they crossed the limits of the forest and went to the city. They saw many things there, tall buildings, vehicles causing pollution, people in a race to earn their daily bread, small children busy with their studies and their games, noise—noise—and more noise.

They started remembering their house. They had become very tired. They were longing for water and some moist, wet place where they could rest a little. Searching for such a place, they entered the shop of a milk seller. They saw a bucket there. They thought that there must be water in it. They both jumped high and reached inside the bucket. But what was this! There was no water in it. It was full of cream. The poor frogs started drowning in the cream, they started suffocating and panting and their eyes started rolling out.

One frog thought, "The end of my life has come. What a destiny I had! Did I have to come to the city and die amongst these strange people?" He thought of his God and started waiting for death. However, the other frog was not willing to accept defeat. He started trying to somehow come out of that cream filled bucket. He started kicking with full force. Despite his great effort, he used to slip down. Even then he did not feel depressed and did not give up courage. He continued trying and kept moving his legs.

And then what was this! Suddenly, he saw that he was rising up. Because of his continuous moving of legs, the cream was also continuously moving and it started changing into butter. The frog saw a ray of hope. He had become very tired, yet he continued kicking. Butter continued to be churned and ultimately, climbing on that butter, the courageous frog started rising up. When the butter started floating on the milk, then that brave frog jumped out of the bucket.

Because of his courage, hard work and the desire to live, the frog was saved but the pessimistic frog drowned in that bucket of cream and died.

Everybody has to face difficulties in his life but God has given us the strength to combat them too.

Hence, one must use that strength to maintain one's courage. Ultimately, it is only the person who does not accept defeat, succeeds. More intelligence or strength are not the only ones that come in handy. Those with courage win the struggle of life.

If you are given an orange and you squeeze it with all your might, then what will come out of it? You think right—'juice'. Do you know why the juice came out when you squeezed the orange? The juice came out of the orange because it had only juice within it. Similarly, how we behave when circumstances are not favourable, when the state and conditions are not comfortable, actually show us what our real or true character is.

Are we able to behave well even under adverse situations? Are we able to keep our temper under control? If yes, then it means that we have learnt the art to keep our mental switch on. There is nothing great about feeling happy when everything is going alright, but keeping your switch on under adverse circumstances is a sign of a tough character.

We must learn the art of keeping our switch on from children. You must have seen how many times small children fall down in a day, but they do not keep lying down. On the contrary, they stand up very quickly. If small children can do so, then why can't adults like us do so? The big difference between successful and the less successful people is this that when the switch of the successful people trips, they switch it on quickly whereas the other people keep switching off the others' switch when theirs is off.

Everyone falls down but only those, who stand up again, reach their goal. The others, not just keep lying down when they fall, they don't even allow others to stand up and try to make others fall down too. We must beware of such persons and keep our switches on.

Japanese Buying

There is a very good story about these 'Slow and lazy Japanese'. An American farmer sells his cows to a Japanese delegation.

The six-member Japanese delegation went to Texas to buy the cows. The American farmer showed them the cows and told the Japanese that he would give them a good proposal. The proposal was this: if the Japanese choose the cows, then each cow will be a hundred dollars and if the Americans choose, then the price will be $90. The American had hoped for an early decision just like we Indians decide on the spot. However, the Japanese believe that slow and steady wins the race. They went into a conference room for an hour. The American was getting mad with anger and was abusing the Japanese saying that they were very slow in thinking. Ultimately, when the Japanese came out, he became restless and asked what their decision was. The leader of the Japanese, in his broken English, said in a soft voice, "Mr. Bill, we would appreciate if you could choose the cows for us."

American: How many?

Japanese: All

The slow Japanese confirmed the deal and the American, suffering a little loss, had to sell all the cows.

The Decision of the Truth and the Untruth

The king of a state decided that if anyone in his state told a lie, he would be hanged. An old hermit of the state was called and asked, "What is your opinion? I have decided that I will not let telling lies continue. Bless me." The hermit asked, "What will you do? What is the solution to not allow lies to continue?" He said, "Everyday, I will hang one man who tells lies." The hermit said, "Amazing! Because till now, what is the true and what is the untrue has not been decided." The king said that he would argue and consider.

The king said, "That is why I have called you to ask you. We shall do as you tell us to do." That recluse said, "Where will you hang the person?" The king said, "At the gate of the town. Tomorrow morning, on the first day of the new year, one man, who is caught lying, will be hanged there." The recluse said, "Then you shall find me at the entrance gate tomorrow morning. See you there tomorrow and bring your jury along too who can decide what the truth is and what the untruth is." The next day, the gate opened. The hermit entered riding a horse. The king asked, "Where are you going riding on the horse?" The hermit said, "I am going to be hanged." The king said, "Why are you telling a lie? Who is going to hang you?" The hermit said, "If I am telling a lie, then hang me but if you do so then what I have said will turn out to be true and if you do not hang me then you have let a man who told a lie go free."

The king said, "If I let this man go free then he is telling a lie when he says that he is going to be hanged. And if I do not let him go and hang him, then it turns out to be true and my hanging him would turn out to be hanging for the truth. What do I do now?" That hermit said, "Inform me when you take the decision, I will come to be hanged." And he went ahead riding on his horse.

☐

Only by keeping your mental switch on helps in difficult times.

Everyone in this world is searching for happiness and there is only one way of acquiring it – keep a control over your thinking.

4

Whatever I have is Special for Me

"Whatever I have is special for me": this means give value or importance to whatever you have or whatever is with you; respect it and tell him or her that he or she is very special to you. Generally, the biggest reason for the sorrows in the life of a person who is forever complaining is that they always find something lacking in whatever they have. Such people forever feel troubled because they continue to look at those shortages only and so they trouble others too. According to them, "Whatever I have is trash."

The only prescription of life that I understand about staying happy is to 'stay happy and keep others happy.' If you want to remain happy then keep everyone around you—whether they are your wife, children, neighbours, boss, friends, colleagues or any other person—happy and think of ways to keep them happy. If we can keep them happy then our staying happy will become equally easy.

Who are You Labouring for?

Generally, we find one thing lacking in us and that

is to trouble or keep our close people troubled. I generally ask one question at my seminar, "Tell me why you do this labour? For whom do you run in the heat throughout the day?" Most of the times, I get only one reply, "For my family or for my children." And I have full faith that your answer too will be the same but when I ask these people only "tell me who you give the greatest pain or suffering to?" You will be surprised to know that most people's reply is "our family or our wife." What will your reply be? I do not know. Don't you find these two replies contradictory that we trouble those people only the most who we slog the whole day for? Yes, this is the truth. Unknowingly, we give the maximum pain to those who are everything for us.

Many a time, at my seminar I have asked the people, "Suppose at this very moment, there is a terrorist attack and the terrorists hold our family hostage and ask for ransom if we want to see them again, then tell me how many of us will agree to give and how much money? There will probably be no such person who will say leave it. I have no desire to see them again or it's good at least I will be saved the trouble of seeing them every day'. The reply of most of the people will be, "We will agree to pay whatever we can at that time; in fact, we will be prepared to give up our lives too." So I tell these people, "See, till today no such attack has happened on us. We are one of those lucky people who get to meet their families again." Every evening you return home from work. Don't you and your family members feel happy when you see each other safe and sound? Or don't you feel comforted?

Probably, because they stay with us, that is why we do not realize their value. It is my belief that it is very good that something good happens, but seeing good is equally essential. In the same manner, to love your family and work hard for them is a very good thing but letting them know of your feelings is equally important. What is the harm in looking good when we are good? When we do love them then why hesitate to express our love? The one reason that I can figure out is our old ideology to 'love but not express it.' If you are hesitant to say it in as many words, then find some way to let them know that they are special for you and that you have love, respect and regard in your heart for them. If nothing, repeat the line 'Everything that is with me is special for me.' Is this not an easy way to stay happy?

This formula is applicable everywhere—whether it is our body, or family, our work, our job or our country. We must value every such thing that is with us—only then will we be able to whole-heartedly welcome the happiness that is waiting for us. So that this feeling continues to be with us always. It is essential that you give honest answers to the following questions. If you do so then you will be able to understand this feeling fully that 'whatever is with me is special for me.'

1. Make a list of your good habits and virtues.

   ----

2. Make a list of all that you find good in your company.

3. Make a list of all the virtues and good habits of all the members of your family.
(While making the lists, kindly do not pay attention to the vices.)

The above questions do not indicate that there are no shortcomings in us, our place of work or in the members of our family. Neither does it mean that our shortcomings are not told or that efforts should not be made to remove them. No Sir. It only means that in our efforts to remove the shortcomings of what we have, we do not ignore their virtues and importance.

The Story of the Twins

I have a friend who has twins. So long as the children were small, it was alright. However, when they became 7 or 8 years old, he was amazed to see that despite their being twins, their nature was absolutely opposite. One was always happy while the other used to keep crying for one reason or the other. He consulted a psychologist, who suggested that take a good quality, expensive gift for the one who was always crying and for the one who was always happy take something that would irritate him and make him angry; so that there will be an equilibrium—even if it was for a short time! The father bought a big robot for the child who always cried and got it packed beautifully. For the good natured child, he got cow dung packed in a box of sweets. He first went to the room of the crying baby. The moment he removed the curtain, he saw that the child had been already crying only for some reason. As soon as he saw his father, he started crying even more loudly, "Why did father bring such a big box for me? As it is, there is very little space in this room." The father said, "Son, I have brought you a gift." The crying baby said, "Such a big one?" The father said, "Yes, son. I have brought a big one so that you may be happy." Crying baby said, "Okay. Open it." Father had just taken out half the robot from the box, when the crying baby started crying loudly again and said, "Why did you bring a black one? You know very well that I do not like black colour."

The father said, "Son, do not cry. We'll get the colour changed but first see it, at least."

Crying baby: "What is this?"

Father: "Son, this is a robot."

Crying baby: "What does this do?"

Father: "It walks, talks and even dances."

Son: "How?"

The father hits his head and says, "It is our fault. Hence, we only will suffer it. Whenever you want to work it, call out to us, we will wind it."

Crying baby, "Now I shall keep calling out to you the whole day long to come and wind it. One, it is in black colour and then one has to wind it to make it work! And then, why is it so heavy? Who asked you to bring this? You do not love me; that is why you keep getting these kind of things."

Cursing his fate, the father went in the direction of the other room where he had sent the box with the cow dung. When he entered the room of the happy child, he saw that the child was very happy and clapping his hands. Irritated, the father asked, "Did you open the box and see what I had sent?"

The son said, "Yes, father. I saw what you had sent. That is why I am so happy."

Father, "What did you see in it that you are so happy?"

The son said, "Father, you can't fool me. I know very well that if there is dung, then the horse also must be somewhere around only."

Now you only tell me; one finds only shortcomings in the robot and the other has hopes of a horse even in dung. This only shows that being happy is also a habit and being unhappy is also a habit.

□

You are given life only once, but if you live it in the right way, then only one time life is enough.

The greatest worry of some people is this only that they want to be worriless.

5

Don't Worry, Contemplate

Problem is Something that We can do Something About

The biggest problem with most of us is that we want to be without worry or tension. Although I know that it is not possible in this age because we become worriless the day we depart from this world.

It is not a bad thing to have worries but just worrying is a bad thing. Whenever we are worried, then it is clear that we are not doing anything and by not doing anything, worries do not leave us.

> ***Worry is the bandit that eats into one's heart,***
> ***What the doctor can do, what remedy to impart?***
> **—Sant Kabira**

If any barricade comes in the way of a liberated, free mind or flowing water, then it does not get perturbed or angry; instead takes some other path to go out happily. You must also have the similar habit of fighting with difficulties so that when the need arises, you can change your path conveniently.

A restricted mind is defensive, fighter, jealous, sceptic or suspicious and extremely critical. A natural and free mind can look at a large number of possibilities.

It has the humility to learn anything from anybody, has immense tolerance, ability to see circumstances in the right way and has the understanding to guess their right price.

Generally, Worry is of Two Kinds

1. **Constructive Tension**—This tension is essential and such a tension is the mother of inventions and solutions. It is extremely important for the success of any individual or business. If any individual is not confronted with these kind of tensions, then that individual and his business soon moves ahead towards his downfall. Starting of some new business, learning something new, the desire to win some game are examples of creative tensions.
2. **Negative Tension**—This is one tension whose solution is not in our hands. Continuously thinking about such a situation is negative tension. Ruining one's present by remembering incidents of the past is an example of negative tension. After all, what is the use of crying over spilt milk? It would be better not to have a repetition of such a

mistake and if it does happen, and the milk does spilt, then make cottage cheese out of it and enjoy it.

You must have also seen how small flies keep buzzing all around us and divert our attention from other important things. These flies, despite being so small compel us to delay achieving our target. Similarly, such small works like the dripping of a tap at home, abnormal sounds from the car, increasing dampness in a wall, slight cough and cold, must be dealt with immediately so that we can go ahead speedily towards the achievement of our target. If you kill these small flies, then you'll find that to some extent, you have your tensions under control.

2.1 Throw yourself into some such work for which planned contemplation is essential or for which some creative work is needed. Then you will not get any time for tensions.

2.2 Search for some direct solution to solve the tension. I do not know how you solve your problems. However, I can tell you the magical formula that Dean Hawks of the prestigious Columbia College adopts to counsel more than two lakh students including Willis, the father of Career Corporation and inventor of the air-conditioner. On a sheet of paper, write down the following questions and their answers.

2.2.1 **First Step – Think:** What is my tension or problem?

- Honestly speaking, we ourselves are not able to understand why we are tense? If we are able to understand our problems and the reasons for them, then half of them will be solved by itself.
- What is the reason for the problem? For what reason did this problem arise? If we ourselves are at the root of the problem, then what is the point of worrying? If the tension has been created because of others, then it will certainly not get solved by getting worried. However, lack of preparation is generally at the root of most of the problems, and we also contribute to it.

2.2.2 **Second Step – Ask:** What harm can come to us from this? What is the minimum and the maximum harm that can come to me? Now when you start writing this with intelligence or wisdom and neutrality, then many a time you will feel that the problem is not as big as you had thought it out to be or the loss will not be as big as you had earlier felt because you will start understanding the solutions to reduce the loss. In Shakespeare's words, "Wise men never feel sorry for their worries, but laughing, think of how to reduce their losses."

2.2.3 **Third Step – Decide:** What can I do to remove the problem or reduce the loss that comes from it. Write down all the alternatives together. Then, select the one you consider the best or if you are confused, select two or three alternatives because any work that we do in time, then whether it is absolutely correct or not, it is 'a little' correct.

2.2.4 **Fourth Step – Act Fast:** Once you reach some decision, start acting on that decision immediately. Do not stop for reconsideration. Contemplation beyond limits can also create confusion. Do not care for 'What will happen now?'

> ***Remember; God does not work for us, instead He works with us.***

Place the Problems in the Right Perspective

Problems help you to move forward, in order to develop in life. Consider problems as medicine or look upon them as fertilizers. A difficulty is a golden opportunity for you to test your capability and determination. "Fortune and misfortune are like the interlocked strands of a rope", this old saying befits the ups and downs of not only business but also our personal lives. It is not enough to only tolerate these difficulties. You should be able to accept these failures as a lesson for the future and try to change every misfortune into good fortune. Till such time as we are in human form, we cannot escape these difficulties. Facing difficulties directly is the only art of solving them. Do not leave anything that has come into your hands. Do something before they get out of hand.

If people do not make an effort towards improvement, then God will also not do miracles for them. God helps those who help themselves.

Fear is such a thing which has benefits but also has disadvantages. If people did not have fear in their minds, then they would have put their hands into the fire and burnt themselves. Also, he would not have hesitated to do the worst kind of crime. We have often seen that because of this fear only, many people are not able to do their work properly. They are forever feeling scared that someone may call their work bad. If we look at things then there are two opinions about each and every work. Some people consider it correct and some consider it wrong. Then how can a decision be taken about right and wrong? Conservative people tell us to walk on the footsteps of their forefathers but if that is done then we cannot make any progress. It has been said that "cars and unworthy sons tread the established path; whereas the three—the poet, the lion and the worthy son set their own paths." The worthy son sets his own path and makes progress. Then how can we decide what is right and what is wrong? Each one of us will have to ask that in our own minds. That is why someone has said, "Whether your mind is clear or not, ask your heart; then do whatever you have to do with happiness."

Generally, people are scared of something or the other. Some are scared of illness or death while some people start feeling scared to see those people who have to face some difficulty, hoping that such a difficulty may not surround them. We must think that nothing is in our hands. Every human being wants to live a secure and happy life, without any difficulty, but he is not aware of what the future has in store for him.

When there is an earthquake or some other natural calamity, we see that some have a miraculous escape and some get perished in that. We are surprised about how some children come out alive from that debris? How did they stay alive without food or water for so many days? What was the power that kept them alive for so long?

Here, I would like to tell you of an incident. Once a human being saw a messenger of the God of Death going. When asked, he said that he was going to get the souls of a hundred people from Benaras. However, it was seen that one thousand people died in Benaras. When the messenger of the God of Death was coming back, the same man met him and asked him that he had gone to get the souls of only one hundred men, then how did one thousand die there? At this, the messenger said that he had taken only one hundred lives, the rest had died because of fright.

I had read a similar incident that a few people were staying in a public lodging (Dharmashala) in the hills. That night, there was a massive storm. The storm was a great dust storm and the trees were moving in such a way that it seemed they would get uprooted. There was loud thunder. It was a scene of annihilation. Everyone was struck with terror and all kind of thoughts were coming into their minds.

They did not even know whether they would be able to see the next day or if this stormy night would be their last night. In this situation of turmoil, one person saw that they were thirteen in number and thirteen is considered a very inauspicious number.

Certainly, one of us is a sinner. Why should all of us die because of that one person? It was the correct thing too, hence, everyone understood it. But, how would one come to know who that sinner was? Each one of them had committed one sin or the other, but none of them thought that this could be the result of his sin.

One who dies in such a dreary night would be a really big sinner. There was a very tall and high tree close to that inn and thunder falls first on tall trees only.

Hence, after a lot of deliberations it was decided that each one of them would stand under the tree alone, for a certain time. Only the person who was destined to die, would die. Why should all of us die for that one person? But, who would be the first to go? Each one of them was afraid whether all this was happening because of his sins.

In the end, it was decided to prepare 13 chits. Each one would take one slip and then go and stand at his position. This having been decided, each one started going according to his number and 12 of them returned without any mishap. They were all happy that all this was not happening because of their sins.

It was now the turn of the 13th person and everyone had full faith that it was this sinner only because of whom their lives had been at risk and that man was also very scared that his life had come to an end. The moment he went and stood there, there was great thunder and the roof of the inn collapsed. All the people under it died instantly.

□

F	—	***False***
E	—	***Experience***
A	—	***Appearing***
R	—	***Real***

If you stay in the marsh, you will never learn how to swim.

6

Locks of Wrong Notions

A good friend is not one who is willing to die for you, but one who can save you too.

One man has written a book in America that 13 is an unlucky number and he has written such scientific books that you will say, "Yes, he is absolutely right." It is believed that the date 13 is inauspicious. It has been the belief already exist itself. Now to prove it, he found out when, where and how many people had fallen off from the 13th floor. In America, there are many buildings which do not have the 13th floor because no one is willing to live on the 13th floor. It is always the 14th floor after the 12th floor because it is very difficult to give the 13th floor out on rent. Hence, there is no 13th floor. That man has found out where and when who all have fallen off the 13th floor; what all accidents have occurred on the 13th; where all has there been a fire and which ships have sunk on the 13th. What planes have met with an accident on the 13th and how many divorces have taken place on the 13th? He has collected all that and information about how many children have died on the 13th. Now the 13th is a big event. What all has happened on the 13th? He has collected all that has been inauspicious.

He has given a lot of examples in his book. He has given so many statistics that it will seem that the 13th is definitely inauspicious. But if anyone wants, he can collect the same for the 12th too or for the 11th. One can collect whatever information one wants. Life is a very big incident. Innumerable incidents keep happening in it. Life is a big mystery. It has innumerable aspects. If a human being takes sides earlier, then he will find arguments in his favour and collect them. He is prepared from beforehand; he is prejudiced. He will see only what he wants to see. He will be able to see only that. He will look for just that and find it too. And then he will think that he has discovered something. This is no discovery.

Why was a Donkey named an Ass?

You all must be well acquainted with a well known animal. That virtuous animal is found close to us off and on. That animal is called an ass. Can you tell me why that animal was named as 'ass'? When I ask people this question at seminars, then generally the reply of the people is like this: "He does not have brains", "He works without thinking", "He does exactly as you tell him to do," etc.

On this, what I tell people is, "These are all his virtues that you are telling me about. No ass is born with a placard of an ass. Then why do we call him an ass?" Then, after racking their brains for a very long time, they ask me the reason for his naming. My reply to them then is, "Sir, I also do not know why a donkey was named an ass. Believe me, the donkey did not tell me also why he was named an ass. It had to be named something, so they named him 'ass'. Now if any one asks me why I was named Suresh only and why not Amitabh, then what can be the answer to this?" People become quiet with this reply. However, dissatisfaction is clearly visible on their faces because they expect some other reply from me. To satisfy them, I tell them why he was named a 'donkey'. I do not know but why we called him an ass only is like this. In Hindi, he is called a 'gadha' which is made up of two syllables—'ga' and 'dha'. 'ga' we have taken from 'galat' or wrong and 'dha' from 'dharana' that is concept. Now, if we join the two words, then we get 'galat dharana' or 'wrong concept'. A donkey has wrong conceptions about himself and about others too. Hence, he was called gadha or ass. He considers himself extremely intelligent and the others, foolish.

If we consider this explanation of the naming of the ass, true, then the question that arises is that even we have many wrong conceptions—towards ourselves and towards others. We generally know these conceptions as 'mental locks' (or blocks). Some of our concepts are such that they bring about an atmosphere of tension and gloom in our lives as well as the lives of the people around us. It is not that we have put these locks purposely. These come up in our brains because of our culture, the atmosphere around us and our education. Few such locks are there in everybody's minds. However, the concept to be contemplated upon is of the number of locks. There is nothing wrong in having locks but not being able to open them or not being willing to open them is a harmful thing.

There is No Fool in this World

In one such seminar, I said, "Nobody in this world is a fool; don't consider anyone to be a fool." The moment I said this thing, a gentleman stood up and said, "Sir, I do not agree with what you said. Some people are actually foolish." I said, "It could be that a person does not have enough knowledge. He may have less knowledge or no knowledge at all. He may be ignorant but not a fool. According to me, one does not lose respect if one tries to learn anything new. In fact, it is a matter of great shame if one does not learn anything new as anything can be learnt at any age." "No, Sir, there can be foolish people too and there are too. You have not seen the world yet," said the gentleman.

Trying once again, to make him understand, I said, "Sir, even those who are admitted into the lunatic asylum are not foolish. They are only mentally sick. Just as we have bodily fever, they have mental fever. They are not foolish either." However, some people have the Aligarh locks on their brains. It is, probably, difficult to break them and this gentleman also, probably had the Aligarh lock on his brain. He said, "Whatever you might say. There are foolish people." Seeing the paucity of time and not getting involved in any argument, I considered it right to accept the gentleman's argument. He was thrilled at his victory. I said, "After meeting you, I feel that what you are saying is correct. There are foolish people."

Actually, considering any one else foolish is the greatest foolishness. Hence, we must try and open such locks immediately. We must be ready to learn something or the other from every individual. There is no foolish person in this world. Hence, one must consider oneself intelligent but must neither consider anyone else foolish nor make a futile attempt to fool someone.

Generally, We have these Wrong Notions in Our Minds

1. A cow gives milk—A cow does not give milk; it has to be taken out of it and that too drop by drop. Similarly, success, happiness and satisfaction are not achieved by themselves. On the contrary, they have to be achieved with hard work, patience, determination and understanding. We can get only three things without effort and these are birth, death and failure and I don't think anyone wants the last two.

2. A patriot is one who can die for one's country—Don't you think we should encourage our soldiers not to die for the country but to kill for the country? One can serve one's country better by staying alive. This does not mean that those who die for the country are not patriots. What I mean to say is that they must have the insanity to kill the enemy—and not to 'die'.

These days, one can see this message written on the walls while going from one place to another—"If you have to live for your country then learn to die." I cannot understand how you will serve your nation by dying? A war is won not by dying but by killing.

3. Kalyug is going on—No, this is the *Karmayug*—the one who will work hard, will keep his concepts clear, will make progress. Today, our children and we have innumerable opportunities and conveniences before us. We decide our future ourselves whereas in earlier times, this convenience was not there. A king's son was a king only and that of a carpenter would be a carpenter only and that of a farmer, a farmer. It is not so today. We have before us, incidents of the success of great men like Atal Bihari Vajpayee, A.P.J. Abdul Kalam, M.S. Oberoi, Dhirubhai Ambani, etc. These and many more such names are enough to negate such a misconception that this is the age of 'Kalyug'. We must break such kind of locks.

4. I have a very bad fate—People who have such locks on their minds consider themselves victims of circumstances and poor and helpless and feel that everyone except them is responsible for it. For every problem, they have only one answer that they are ill-fated. To find the key to such a lock is a little difficult. Whenever such people wake up late, they always find a traffic jam on the road, they miss their bus or the car doesn't start, they get a scolding from the boss—all because 'they have bad luck'; while we all know pretty well that it is not our luck which is bad but the habit of waking up late which is bad; the car is not working because we do not get it serviced in time; the boss is not bad, it is our habit to postpone the work which is bad. Instead of looking for our shortcomings, we have got used to putting all the blame on fate. The result is that we keep repeating the same mistakes throughout our lives because instead of taking on the responsibility for it, we keep blaming our fate.

Sheep or Lion

A new born lion fell in the midst of a flock of sheep. He brought him up and he started thinking that he was a sheep. He started walking like a sheep in his flock. He would get frightened like them and eat grass and leaves. One day a lion happened to see him and he was amazed how the sheep, without getting frightened, was walking with a lion. The lion jumped between the sheep. Seeing this, the sheep started running helter skelter. The lion, who had grown up amongst the sheep also started screaming and ran. The lion caught him and pulling him, said, "Foolish! You are not a sheep, you are a lion." But, how could he agree? He thought there was something fishy in it; because this was contrary to his whole life's experience.

The other lion was also, after all, a lion. He pulled this lion and took him to a pond. He shouted a lot, cried but contrary to his desire, the other lion continued pulling him towards the pond and saying, "You foolish person! Look at your face and mine in the water. Do you see any difference? You are exactly the same as I am." Frightened, the lion looked. He felt as if he was dreaming because we consider only what we have seen many times to be the truth. Anything new seems like a dream. He couldn't believe it, so he looked again. His whole life's experience was that he was a lamb.

> ***If you change your vision, then the scenes will change;***
> ***If you change your direction, then the condition will change;***
> ***If you change your habits, then your stars will change.***

To make him feel reality, the lion roared. Hearing his roar and seeing his face clearly in the mirror, the sleeping lion in the young lion woke up and then he started living like a lion only.

We all are like the sleeping lion too. We also have a lot of talent and possibilities hidden within us, but some of us keep crying over our fate and keep avoiding valour. If anyone tries to wake us up or inspire us, we keep avoiding it by saying that "This malady is not under our control." This is nothing but a lock on our minds that success comes only if you are fated to get it.

5. Had the cat taught the lion to climb up a tree, then the lion would have eaten the cat—This thinking of ours exhibits our feeling of not wanting to teach anyone anything. This reveals the fear hidden inside us whereby, in order to safeguard our position, we never teach anyone under us, so much that our position gets endangered. I, however, feel that if the cat had taught the lion how to climb a tree, then she would herself, probably have learnt how to fly. You are all aware that necessity is the mother of all inventions. Hence, in order to save her life, the cat would definitely have learnt something new. If you do not even agree to the cat thing, you will definitely agree that if he wants, man can continuously learn something new. If we learn continuously, then it will lead to the progress or prosperity of the entire society. It will benefit all of us because we will all be learning something new.

6. Responsibility is a burden, which has to be carried—I have said quite a lot about this before also. Now, all I'll say is that if this responsibility had been a burden, we would have unloaded it a long time back or thrown it away; but it is our strength which keeps giving us the inspiration to continuously keep doing something or the other. Besides, if we fulfil our responsibilities happily, then they never seem like a burden.

7. My religion is the correct one, the others are wrong—Our biggest and the most dangerous lock is towards religion. When we talk of religion, we are ready to kill and be killed. All our understanding collapses when we come to this issue. However generous or open minded a person may seem to be, when it comes to religion, he starts seeming to be completely different. It would be better if we do not get entangled on this fact and waste our precious time.

It is not time now to know which the oldest or best religion is but to know to which direction we are taking our children's future. Will it not be proper that we continue believing in our own religion and let others continue believing in whichever religion they have belief in.

Money is the Root of All Evil

January 8, 2006 was the coldest day in 70 years in the history of Delhi. Newspapers carried the news that 150 people had died because of the cold. Every year we read news of people dying because of heat stroke. I do not think that these people died because of the cold or the heat. This is only an excuse for their death. The actual reason is 'poverty' meaning scarcity of money.

Millions of people in this world die because of such diseases as can be cured by even ordinary medicines. But they either do not have the strength to buy the medicines or nobody gives them information about these medicines or supplies to them; because they are poor. Today, science has made such progress that even an individual with a heart disease can be saved and is being saved. But, even today, people in our country are dying because of fever, cough, etc. Even today, millions of children die before they are born or get killed while being born, why? Because, due to shortage of money, they do not have access to the basic conveniences.

Even today, there is no dearth of such news that parents sell off their children for just a little amount of money or make them work from a very young age. Human beings are acting in such a manner as probably animals also would not do and that too because of shortage of just a few rupees.

Shri A.P.J. Abdul Kalam, former President of our country, has rightly said that the biggest enemy of India, at present, is poverty. Till such time that the demon of poverty is not destroyed from the roots, corruption, terrorism, illiteracy, communalism, etc. will continue to be harvested. If we go deep into any problem, then we will find that the root cause is 'poverty'.

I certainly do not mean that the poor do all the wrong acts. In fact what I am saying is that they only are target to all kinds of diseases, natural calamities, illiteracy and terrorism; because they do not have money. Hence, it is essential that we accept this epidemic of poverty as a disease and cooperate with every Indian to free it from this disease so that our country can, once again, become the golden bird; where everyone can live with respect, mutual love and brotherhood.

Come, let us get together to make India a content, healthy and prosperous country so that we can look the forthcoming generation in the eye and say that we have created this India with our hard labour.

□

Wrong notions towards ourselves, towards people and towards circumstances is the biggest lock of our minds.

Every Work is Difficult Before it Becomes a Habit.

7

Habits—with Life, Even after Life

Habits are with life because they only determine the direction of our life. And they are even after our lives because these habits only get transferred into our children and determine the condition and direction of their lives. Hence, it is very essential that we have the correct habits. My scale of judging our habits is very simple, which is like this....

Any such habit which you do not want to see in your children should not be present in you. Try to inspect yourselves before giving instructions to your children or teaching them some things, to see if you have the right to give them those instructions? Try to test your habits on that scale.

We give birth to children but probably in our run of life, forget to give them the correct upbringing. Correct and right upbringing does not mean making costly or expensive education, costly clothes, costly hobbies or costly toys available to them but also with good habits. According to me, the way we give all our property and indebtedness into our children, we probably do not even feel that and if we do feel it, then it is late. Habits are a part of our cultures. Hence, inculcate good habits in the form of culture. Children do not do what you tell them to do. In fact, they do what they see you doing. Hence, take care of the way you behave, present the best example before them and be prepared to sacrifice some essential relaxations.

Slave to Habits

In order to capture a monkey, the conjurer places a small cage, shaped like a paw, in the forest with a few peanuts in it. With the greed for the peanuts, the monkey climbs down the tree and the moment he puts his hand into the cage to get the peanuts, it closes. This is how the monkey's paw gets caught in it. However, the hole of the cage is so big that if he drops the peanut from his hand then he can straighten his hand and pull it out. But the monkey does not leave the peanut and he remains caught. Whenever I narrate this incident in my seminar, the audience pities the foolishness of the monkey. The monkey is an animal. He does not have the brains to understand greed or good and bad. We consider ourselves to be the most 'intelligent' animal but sometimes, behave like the monkey. For example, we all know that cigarette, *gutkha*, alcohol, etc. are bad things; they harm our health which can create great difficulties for our family, yet, like the monkey, we continue holding on to those habits and stay away from the fruits of health and prosperity.

We must awaken and become aware of our habits. Do not leave anything for tomorrow and do it today. We give such habits to our children as legacy. Will any parent want to give his child a rotten apple? If not, then why should we give our children bad habits?

Today, people are very wakeful towards the security of their children's future. They buy various kinds of life insurance policies. This is a very good thing. But if you really want to secure their future, then give them good habits in legacy, teach them how to set high targets and how to achieve them. And the beginning towards this will have to be made by setting an example before them and not lecturing them or scolding them.

Strength of the Hands

I saw a scene while coming to office. I had seen that scene many times before, but had probably not paid attention to it and that was that a massive elephant had been tied to the trunk of a tree with a very thin rope. When I saw that elephant, a question arose in my mind that despite being so huge and powerful, why is this elephant so helplessly tied with this thin rope. It was my stern belief that if the elephant wanted, it could break this rope. Then why does it not break it? To quench this curiosity of mine, I asked the mohout of the elephant, "Brother, what is the secret of this miracle? How do you keep such a big elephant under your control? Does it not try to escape?" He said, "He had tried many times to free himself when he was small. At that time, we used to tie him with thick iron chains. But despite millions of efforts, it could not free itself. Slowly, it reduced its efforts and finally, completely stopped. Now the rope is weak but he feels that this also will not break and so he remains tied." Hearing his reply, lightning seemed to flash through my brain. I felt that probably our psyche had also become like the elephant's. We also remain tied to our bad habits and think that breaking away from them is very difficult. Similarly, many people say, "I want to give up smoking but cannot or I want to wake up early but can't." When I hear this statement, I am reminded of that elephant who, being a slave to these wrong thoughts, spends his entire life by being tied with this ordinary rope.

For a person who wants to work, work never ends. There is always a new work ready for him.

Recognise the Changed Circumstances, the Boiled Frog

The Chinese people eat frogs. To eat this, they used to first heat up the water, then they used to put live frogs into it; but what used to happen was that the frogs used to immediately jump out because of the heat of the water. But now, they first put the frogs into ordinary water. When they start swimming in it, then they slowly start heating the utensil on slow fire. What is amazing in this is that the frog does not even come to know when it gets cooked. Do you know the reason for this? The reason is: the frog slowly starts adapting to the increasing heat and by the time he gets to know of the seriousness of this thing, it is too late. Hence, it is very essential that we continuously keep making good changes within ourselves and keep new things for our own development. We must, consciously try not to fall prey to any wrong habit. If we do not recognize the changing circumstances and the pulse of time, then we can change to ashes like the frog. Mostly people fall prey to their habit of laziness and are unable to make any progress in life even though they do not have any dearth of brilliance or opportunities.

I feel that if man wants then he can leave any habit in a moment, but only if he determines to do so. Not just the desire; the difficulty comes in when we only have the desire but do not set any targets. We want changes in our circumstances without changing our habits. Can this be possible? Yes. This can happen but only with a miracle. Losing this invaluable life in the hope of a miracle will not be a very sensible thing, therefore it will be good if we are aware of our habits, take the responsibility for our condition and our direction on ourselves and do not have only the desire to improve on our habits but also make it our target.

Follow the Principle of 'I want' Instead of 'Have to' in Life

I have seen that some people feel happy going to

work while some people do not like to go to work and they stay unhappy for some reason or the other, although there is no difference in the earnings of the two of them. If the family circumstances are also nearly the same then also, some people stay happy in both—the workplace and the home and keep the people around happy too. But some people's lives are always spent in irritation, dissatisfaction and complaints, etc.

Such people always have complaints and dissatisfaction with life. They always find fault with their work, their company, themselves, their families and they find something lacking in everything. They are always troubled themselves and trouble others too. I have learnt from my own experience that the main difference, besides our works, is their way of living, their thinking and their negative attitude towards circumstances.

Is it their helplessness or compulsion? Any work that you may say can be done as a compulsion or a necessity. However, if you do it as a compulsion, then you will not be able to enjoy the process of the work and if you do it considering it to be a necessity, then you will not only be able to enjoy the work, the work will not even seem like a burden to you.

At a seminar, I advised people that they should take their families for an outing on holidays if they want to have a happy family life. One gentleman probably did not like this advice of mine. He said, "What are you saying? As it is I am pressed with hard work for six days; on top of that you say that I should take my family for an outing on a holiday too."

To him, I said in a very polite way, "After all, why do you go to work to be pressed? I do not understand how anyone goes willingly to get continuously pressed. Does your company ring you up every day and call you from home?" He said, "No". Then I said to him, "Don't you think you go to work at your own will. Nobody compels you to come. That means you go to get pressed at your own sweet will. Then whose fault is it? If someone else is employed instead of you or if someone else is willing to take your children for an outing, then, do you think you will feel good?" The gentleman became speechless at this.

What we need to do is change our way of thinking. We must remove 'have to' and change it to 'want to'. This will help you experience happiness in your life. There are some works in life which we have to do but if we do those works happily, then those works will not be done under compulsion but will be done in happiness.

The Habit of Eating a Lot

A lady came to her mother's house. Her husband also came to fetch her. When he started eating, he used to eat one whole *puri* in one morsel only. Those who were feeding him were upset—the moment they gave him a *puri,* it would vanish in a minute. The wife was watching all this quietly. She started feeling embarrassed about what people would think about the kind of husband she had got. Seeing no one else there, she indicated to her husband with two fingers that he must break the *puri* into two pieces and eat them. The husband thought that his wife was telling him to eat two *puris* together. His wife banged her head. When they spoke to each other, the wife said, "You were the limit. You were alright in the beginning only. One doesn't eat one *puri* in one morsel but just I tried telling you that with signs that you must break the *puri* into two, you started eating two in one morsel only."

The husband said "You probably do not know of which family we come. I am nothing. Whenever my late father went to anybody's house to eat, he had to be brought back home in a bullock-cart. Once his condition became so bad that he had to somehow, be brought back home. Then, the moment the *vaidya* (doctor), came and gave him a pill, he opened his eyes and said, 'Vaidyaraj, if I had space for this in my stomach, would I have not eaten another *laddoo*? There is no more space in my stomach.'"

The Habit of Asking for a Little More

Dhabbooji came to a *paan* shop one day and asked him to prepare a *paan* for him. He asked the man to put a little more tobacco. Then he asked him to put a clove and a little stronger peppermint. He did as he was told. Then, he said, "Friend, you forgot to put the *gulkand*. The man put a little *gulkand* also. "Now put a cardamom too so that one can get some taste at least." When he put the cardamom, Dhabbooji, once again said, "Listen, if you have a little *Paan Bahar* too, then put a little of that too." The shopkeeper could not bear it any more. In anger, he said, "Now, Sir, if you order then I shall put this 25 paisa coin of yours into this *paan*."

□

A step becomes a stair only when one climbs the stairs; before that, it is only a stone. Till such time that one does not climb on it, it cannot be called a stair. It becomes a stair only when it is climbed over. Some unintelligent and stupid people make stones out of stairs too. And some intelligent people climb over stones also and make them steps.

One Kind Word Can Change Someone's Entire Day.

8

The Power of Words and of Focus

Words and Thoughts Influence Each Other

While speaking, always bear in mind that if these words are my last words, then what will people think about me. Just as Mahatma Gandhi's last words were 'Hey Ram', these words are still embossed on his grave. Had his last words been 'Hai Ram', then think what could have happened? Hence; choose and use words carefully. Our tongue can prove to be our greatest friend or foe. The same tongue can bless or curse—that depends on you.

The tongue told the teeth, "Please be careful, I am inside. Don't bite me." The teeth told the tongue, "I will take care of you, but you take care that I don't get broken."

If a person understands the art of conversation or if he learns it, then the chances of his becoming successful will be greater than those of others.

> ***Probably God also cannot accept strictness in our talk; that is why He did not give a bone to the tongue.***

In this sequence only I am reminded of a song which we have been listening to since our childhood:

"Hum honge kaamyaab, Hum honge kaamyaab, Hum honge kaamyaab ek din; man mein hai vishwaas, pura hai vishwaas, Hum honge kamyaab ek din"

(We shall succeed, we shall succeed, we shall succeed one day: There is faith in my mind, complete faith, that we shall succeed one day.)

I remember, from approximately from Class IV, we used to sing this song at our morning assemblies and reached Class XII singing this song only. One day, I asked my friend, "Since Class IV, we have been singing 'We will be successful one day', after all when will we be successful?" At this, my friend's reply was, "Just keep singing this song without objecting because our fathers also used to sing this song. This is only a song. Has anyone ever acquired success by singing songs?"

Don't you think we've got into the habit of singing such songs as reflect only laziness and not inspiration? You can see an example of this on the last day of the year, that is 31 December, when people sit down with an exercise book and a pen and note down their resolutions for the coming year such as "Shall stop drinking and smoking from January 1"; "Shall start morning walks from January 1"; "Shall start studying seriously from January 1," etc. and by the time January 7 comes, these resolutions are forgotten. Then starts the process of excuses such as "January 1 is the beginning of the New Year according to the British, the New Year of us Indians starts on the 14th of April. Hence, we sit down with a paper on the 13th of April and by the time we reach April 20, always in the same position. However, we do not lose hope and then find happiness in realizing that four months have already been crossed. Now, let January come again and our life goes on like this. I have heard people say that "I am going to give up drinking from tomorrow, so come, let us finish all the bottles today or, I am giving up smoking from tomorrow, so let us smoke all the packet tonight itself." Hence, we will do everything from tomorrow only and nothing today. All changes will be made tomorrow only and nothing today.

The 'one day' in the song "We shall overcome...." Probably doesn't ever come in our lives. If any work can be done, it cannot be done today or ever happen. So replace these words with "Today and from now."

Thanks and Forgiveness—An Easy and Successful Way

You are all aware that if a machine is kept in proper condition for a long time, then it requires servicing from time to time. If the machine is not serviced from time to time, then its life is shortened. Our human relations, sometimes reach the breakdown point with time because of our wrong habits. However, if at the right time, we use the correct words like 'Thank You' and 'Sorry', then the tension that is born in relations can be ended at that time only. It is the suggestion of some foreign Fire Fighting Department that 80% of the frightful fires of the world can be controlled if one can put one cup of water at the right place at the right time. However, once the fire breaks out, even a dozen of fire fighting engines find it difficult to bring it under control. Along with this, if words like 'Thank You' and 'Sorry' are said in the right expression, then this is a very effective and easy way to build cordial relationships.

> ***The irony of life is not that people cannot achieve their targets, but the fact that they do not have any targets.***

Saying 'Thank You' to Your Wife

I was talking to people at a seminar and telling them that I thanked my wife for giving me a glass of water and even food. I had just said this when a gentleman stood up and said. "Sir, you have been telling us very nice things since morning. It feels very good. But what are you saying now? You thank your wife for giving you a glass of water also?" I said, "Yes, it is true." He said, "This is no special work. Every wife does this work."

I said, "Sir, the special thing is that every wife gives water to her own husband. To me, only my wife gives water." He asked, "What is this you are saying." I explained my statement to him in very clear words, "See, Sir, my wife takes care of me and all members of the family. She takes care of the children and does many other household works. My wife feels happy when I just say these two words in exchange for all the work she does."

The gentleman could not digest this. In a little softer voice, he said, "What is so great about this? She stays at home the whole day long." In order to make him understand, in a jovial tone, I said, "How will you feel if after you go out for work, your wife does not stay at home?" He probably understood it this time and he sat down quietly. Once again, to have some fun, I said, "Sir, now you definitely need to thank your wife." He asked, "Why?" I said, "Because, despite having a husband like you, she stays at home the whole day."

> ***The greatest sorrow for any parent is when he/ she sees some wrong habit of theirs in their child.***

The Power of FOCUS

Once a child asked his mother, "Mother, what is the best and easiest way to make someone happy?" The mother said, "I will tell you this later, first go and ask your grandfather how he is feeling." The son went to the grandfather and asked, "Grandfather, how are you feeling?"

The grandfather said, "Son, I am not feeling good. My whole body is aching and the pain in my knee just refuses to go." The pain was clearly visible on the grandfather's face. The child went back to his mother and repeated his question, "Mother what is the easiest and best way to give someone happiness?" Without giving any reply, the mother said to her son and said, "First, go to your grandfather again and ask him, 'Which were the happiest days of your life?' Then I shall give you an answer to your question."

The son went to his grandfather once again and asked grandfather the question his mother had asked him to utter. Hearing the question, grandfather closed his eyes and when he opened his eyes, there was a wave of happiness on his face, and brightness and enthusiasm were clearly visible in his eyes.

He said, "I felt a peculiar kind of happiness the first time I touched you, the first time that your father addressed me as 'papa' and took the first step to walk; when you and I used to go for walks. At those times, I used to feel as if I was the luckiest person of this world."

Seeing the sudden change on grandfather's face, the child was amazed and went back to his mother and told her the entire story. After hearing this, the mother said to her son, "Have you now got an answer to your question?"

The child said, "But you have not given any reply yet." While making the child understand it, the mother said, "See son, an easy way to give happiness to anybody is 'The right words and the right focus'. This means that you will get the same reaction as the kind of words you use. You will get the same answer as the question you ask. Hence, concentrate on the words that you use."

"When you asked your grandfather about his health, you made him focus on his pain and you could see the pain on his face; but when you asked him about his moments of happiness, then, despite being sick, his face blossomed with happiness. This means that pleasant thoughts started coming to his mind and he started looking happy."

I also feel that one problem is very effective. The kind of words/questions we use, the same kinds of thoughts are created and our attention goes to those kind of things only. An example of this is the crying people, the frightened people and the laughing people at a cinema hall. Despite knowing that it is only a matter of light and shade, we get involved in it. If we, by being aware of it, use this process to improve our relationships and use the right questions and answers by making use of the focus of our attention properly, then we also can bring about a great change in our lives.

'Question' is the fastest way to change the focus. If you ask better questions yourself, then you get better replies. The question you ask yourself strengthens your focus. Jesus Christ says, "Ask and you shall be answered."

Four questions have been given on the next page, answers to which can prove helpful to change your focus.

What are you happy about? (Things which we have with us or things without which it is impossible to be happy. For example, healthy body, employment and family, etc.)

- -

- -

- -

- -

- - - - - - - - - - - - - - - - - -

What do you feel proud about? (Such works or achievements which you have acquired on your own with your own hard work.)

- -

- -

- -

- -

- - - - - - - - - - - - - - - - - -

Which people do you feel grateful to? (Such people who may sometime or the other, have helped you in some way or the other.)

- -

- -

- -

- -

- - - - - - - - - - - - - - - - - -

Who do you love? Who loves you?

- -

- -

- -

- -

- - - - - - - - - - - - - - - - - -

If you answer these questions honestly, then you will find whether your attitude towards life is positive or not.

□

Many things in this world cannot be seen or touched, they can only be felt by the heart.

When you start talking about your achievements more than your targets, then understand that you have become old.

9

Get into the Habit of not Just Having Desires, But Also Setting and Achieving Targets!

Once a passenger, while crossing a crossroad, asked a person, "Which road should I take?" The man said, "Where do you want to go?" The passerby said, "I do not know." The man answered, "In that case, you can go on any path." People without a target become directionless.

If wishes were horses, beggars would ride. But in life, one cannot achieve anything with desires only. On the contrary, we need to acquire them and that too, in drops. Till today, I have not found a man who does not want to stay happy, who does not want to keep his family happy, does not want to become rich, who does not want to be successful.

"Everyone wants everything, but does not get it." And the main reason for this is that they just desire it. They neither make it the target of their lives nor do they take any necessary step to acquire it. The limit is that they do not want to bring about any change.

Actually, most of the people do not understand the difference between desire and target and if they do understand, then they just set targets but are not able to labour or make as much sacrifice as is required to achieve it. They give up in the middle of the road only and convince themselves by giving any excuse—whether it be destiny or dearth.

It is essential to have the following virtues to convert desires into targets—

- Direction
- Dedication
- Discipline
- Deadline

Direction—The first condition for the achievement of any kind of target is to have a plan. It is not essential that the plan be the best, only then we should start it. It is necessary to have a plan and a direction. Don't consider the best to be an enemy of better and whatever plan you have prepared can be started only with the first step.

Dedication—The second important step for the achievement of the target is the presence of devotion and dedication. This means that one must have the aim to achieve the target somehow or the other and that we are prepared for any effort or sacrifice required for it. If we do not feel any repentance at not achieving our target, then it is quite clear that it was just our desire and not our target. If our desire is fulfilled then it gives us happiness, but if it is not fulfilled then it does not give us any sorrow. However, targets have to be achieved or else we feel unhappy. For example,

"I want to become the Prime Minister of India." If this happens somehow, then it will give me happiness; but if I do not become the Prime Minister, then it will not make me unhappy because I did not make any effort to achieve it.

Discipline—Discipline means self-control, ownership of oneself. There are many definitions of discipline but the one thing that is most important in these is that 'essential works' definitely have to be done and not do at all the works that are unimportant. We generally see that people are very busy but in such unimportant works as has nothing to do with their lives. For example cricket, Indian Idol or wasting time in discussing politics. Instead of being attracted towards activities that give us short-term happiness but long-term unhappiness, we must do activities that give us long-term benefits. Even if it be painful initially, but it is a part of discipline. Generally, it is because of this lack of discipline only and not being able to have any control over our raw greed that people falls short of achieving their target.

Deadline—If time limit is not added to the desire, then it does not get converted to the target. It is also true that tension is created because of the time limit but this is creative. It is because of this time limit only that we use our extra ability and courage to do the work. It is my belief that marriages also take place because of this, because wedding cards carry the date of the wedding or else these marriages would also get postponed.

More			
Desire	Thinkers	winners	
	Vegetables	Animals	More
	Work		

In this way, there are a few people who set targets in life but lack the courage and the determination that is required to achieve it, are not able to procure it. This thing can be easily understood from the sketch given above.

1. Vegetable: Such people and do not have a target in their lives and do not have any direction or speed either. Such people continue to live only because they have not died. According to me, they are living a life like vegetables.

2. Animal: Such people talk a lot but do not know their targets or the purpose of their work. Such people are living definitely, but why? They do not know. You must also definitely have seen some dog suddenly starts barking and chasing some scooter or motor cycle on the roads and if the driver of the vehicle stops then they go back whimpering. I do not understand, if he does not have any work with the vehicle or its driver, then why does he bark and chase the vehicle? Probably, because it is an animal; because he is not aware of the purpose for which he ran after the vehicle.

3. Thinkers: Such people who know everything about what the purpose or target of their work is: how it is to be achieved and also know that it is true how difficult it is to set targets. However, the hard work and sacrifices that are required to achieve this, we are not able to do that. They have that knowledge about what is right and what is wrong, but what is amazing is that what is done is done by only those who do wrong. Such people do not have any scarcity of knowledge but they do not make use of it in their own lives.

Thinkers in Military

During the First World War, an American thinker got recruited in the Army. It is the job of a thinker to think. He knows only one work—think, think. When he joined the military, he was absolutely healthy, there was no stopping him. The doctors gave him permission. All the parts of the body, in fact, the whole body was alright. His eyes were alright, he was competent in every way, but no doctor could, in the wildest of his dreams, imagine that a completely physically fit man was incapable of doing anything except think. How could it be known after seeing him also? Neither you, nor anyone else would have been able to know this. He got recruited into the army and on the first day itself, when he stood in the line, the teacher who had come to train him said, "Left turn", all the soldiers turned to the left, but he stood straight. The teacher said, "Sir! Can you not hear?"

He said, "I can hear very clearly, but I cannot do anything without thinking. I am thinking whether I should turn to the left or not." His teacher said, "In that case, there is great difficulty. If you think so much then it will become very difficult for you to go ahead on this soldier's life. Tried a lot to make him understand but there was no way. He would not do anything without thinking.

And if he had done anything after thinking, it would have been alright but he used to think so much that the time to do anything would lapse and in thinking, new thoughts used to get created; and there was no end to the series. Later, we got to know that this gentleman had wanted to marry and had even proposed to some lady. He kept thinking for three years in favour and against it. Even after three years, he could not decide if getting married was right or not. After three years, he came to the house of that lady to tell her that he was sorry, he had not been able to take any decision. But, by then, the lady had got married and even had three children.

Thinking that the man was of no use but because he had got recruited into the army and was a famous thinker, it was important to employ him in some work or the other. Hence, he was sent to the kitchen of the soldiers. He would be able to do some small jobs there. The first day itself, he was given the task of pealing peas and separating the small and the big peas. After an hour, when his teacher reached near him, he found him sitting with his head between his hands. The peas were just as he had left them. He asked, "Sir, were you not able to do this also?" He said, "I will do it, but let me think. It is clear now that there are both—small and big peas but there are some middle sized ones too. What do I have to do with those and till such time as it is decided what I have to do with them, there is no point in getting into the trouble. I thought a lot about where to put them—with the big peas or the small ones because the middle sized peas are neither small nor big or both."

God knows what happened to that person later on. We can imagine what must have happened to him. However, all of us are also nearly like him on issues of life.

4. Winners: Such people, who establish big targets in life and do not hesitate to carry out as much hard work as is required to achieve the target, such people know that "success cannot be achieved very easily, but it is never costly."

The Characteristics of Target

Specific: The following things are included in specific targets—

- What: What is to be achieved?
- Why: Purpose, reason, benefit?
- How: Needs and difficulties?
- When: What is the time span?
- Where: Place?
- Who: Who is included in the target?

Measurable: Always set such targets, progress from which can be measured and a comparative study of which can be made. Achieving of the target can be made easy by measuring the progress of the target. It helps one to know how close or far one is from achieving one's target.

Achievable and challenging: Your target must definitely be challenging but never desire the impossible; because this way, one gets nothing but disappointment. Always remember that no task is impossible. Always consider the target to be difficult but achievable. Only then can one achieve it. Easy tasks do not have the possibility of progress.

Realistic and worth achieving: Such targets should, in one way or the other, be linked to you, your institution, society and family and after the achievement of the target, at least one of them shall show progress. In order to set a realistic target, you must have faith or belief in that target. In order to give your target realistic form, it is essential to compare that target to previous experiences. Only then can one benefit from it.

A tangible target: Proof of the achievement of the target will definitely be seen or felt. No target is clear till such time that one does not experience it or see its results.

Types of Targets

There are three kinds of targets—

1. Outcome Goal
2. Process Goal
3. Performance Goal

For Example

1. For any bowler, to get the batsman out, is the **outcome goal.**
2. For the achievement of the outcome goal, he will have to concentrate his target on the following **process goal.**
    - To find out the strength or the weakness of the batsman within a certain period
    - To remain physically fit always
3. The **performance goal** a bowler must have will to study about the strength and weakness of a batsman within a definite period of time.
    - On the basis of the information thus gathered, practise those balls on which the batsman generally gets out, for example target five good length balls in one over if the batsman has generally got out on good length balls.
    - Practise eating and exercising regularly so that you remain physically fit. This way, you saw that through the achievement of the process goal, setting of targets and performance goals only can the outcome goal be achieved.

However, here it is essential to say that even if you do achieve the process and the performance goals, you may, sometimes, miss out on the outcome goal because it is possible that by the time the bowler attacks the weakness of the batsman, the batsman may have improved upon his weakness and make it his strength. Hence, what is meant by what is said is that the outcome goal is not in one's hand, but the process and the achievement of the performance goals always depends upon us. Just as explaining to Arjun, Lord Krishna had said in the Gita, "Oh, Arjun! However great a bowman you may be, but your authority is only on your bow, arrow and your power of concentration. You have no authority on the deer which you are aiming at; because it may move at that time." Hence, the wise recognize their area of authority and do not either regret or get tired and give up if they are unable to achieve the outcome goal in one effort. On the contrary, they, once again, set their targets according to the changed circumstances.

People generally ask me if there is a difference between the desire of a successful person and an unsuccessful person? I feel that "the difference is not in the desire but the intensity of the desire." Generally, people have desires but the desire is not so intense that they are willing to sacrifice anything to achieve this. History is witness that only those people have been successful who are not willing to take anything less than success.

The Seven Rules for the Achievement of Success

1. Say only that which you desire; not what you do not desire
2. Make your goal realistic and challenging
3. It should be within the area of your influence and rights

4. Evaluate your progress
5. Examine your resources
6. Assess the prices
7. Reward yourself

□

Children do not do what we tell them to do. On the contrary, they do what they see us doing.

10

Are You a Hero in the Eyes of Your Children/Family?

Do not teach your children cleverness, but it is certain that you will be the first victim.

Are You a Hero?

During a seminar at Jaipur, in which many people had been invited, I called a child sitting in the row before me and asked him—

"What is your name?"

The child replied, "Adesh Shrivastava."

Once again, I asked, "What is your age?"

The child said, "Fourteen years."

I asked, "Adesh, will you tell me who you like the most in this world?"

The child immediately answered "Hritik Roshan."

Once again, I asked, "And in the number two position?"

The child immediately answered, "Sachin Tendulkar."

Again I asked, "At number three?"

"James Bond."

Then I asked the child who he had come there with? The child's father was sitting with him only. He got up very proudly. He felt that he would probably be honoured. I asked him, "Sir, did you not feel strange hearing the replies of your son?" In an amazed style, he said, "No. There was nothing strange." Again, I said, "Even after hearing everything, are you still feeling that everything is alright?"

"Yes, what do you find wrong in this?" I said, "Sir, I had asked your son who he liked the most in this world? I had not asked him who he wanted to be like? I was quite amazed that he did not take your name at the first position; nor in the second position or the third position. I feel that if I had gone upto the 10th position also, he would not have taken your name. I, anyway, did not want to ask more than this." After understanding what I wanted to say, the father glared at his son. It seemed as if in his heart he was saying, "I brought you here, paid for the tickets and you go and take the names of other people. Wait! I'll teach you a lesson!"

Do you not feel that we are unable to remain as heroes in the eyes of our children for very long? What is the reason for this? Are today's children spoilt? I feel that it is generally our behaviour or our habits are the main reason for it. I myself am passing through this experience. Even today, if he is asked who the strongest man in the world is, the reply of my son, Akhil, who is 13 years old, is, "My papa. Who else?" If you say, "Even more than Salman Khan?", his reply is, "Yes, Salman Khan is alright but my father is smarter."

I feel that nearly all children who are about as old as my son, probably consider their fathers to be just that. However, as they grow older, the periphery of their understanding also goes on increasing and their faith, their belief gets shattered: because now they begin to understand the difference between what we say and do.

They get to know that their parents are not as they think and the pain of disappointment gives birth to an unwanted anger which can be clearly seen in the increasing gap between father and son.

I am reminded of an incident from my childhood, which I want to narrate to you. There was an aunt who lived next door. She had two children. Every evening, at about 5:30 or 6, she'd ask her children to go up. One day, a neighbour asked her, "Sister! Please do not mind but for a very long time, I have been wanting to ask you a question for some time. Why do you ask your children to go up every evening?" The aunt replied, "Actually, the thing is that this is the time of his return." Amazed, the neighbour asked, "So what is there to hide from the children?"

In a sad tone, the aunt replied, "Actually, he comes back home very tired and his work at office is quite tension-filled. That makes him quite irritated. You are aware that children do not understand all this. They keep playing and keep making a ruckus around him. Irritated by all this, he sometimes even gives a beating to the children. To escape these everyday problems, I have adopted this method. I send the children here and there before his arrival."

It is clear from this that the image of the husband in this house is not a loving one but a frightening one. What is the use of having such a father come back home wherein the people of his family have to go into hiding or be in terror. I feel that probably this is the reason why some children get fed up of bad behaviour of their parents—a behaviour which is made up of bad habits—and want to grow up fast and free themselves of this suffocating life.

Generally, we are all very honest and love our families and work a lot but are probably not able to convey this properly to our families and the company. For this, some of our own habits are also responsible. This can be explained more clearly with this example—a chef makes the most delicious *kheer* (milk and rice pudding). But at the end of it all, instead of putting almonds and raisins into it, he puts ash; thus making all his efforts go to waste.

This ash is nothing but our behaviour and our bad language, because of which all our efforts go waste and we do not get the fruit that we should have got. Actually, some people sometimes make the mistake of considering the home to be an inn. They go there only to take rest meaning go there in the evening, sleep, get up in the morning and go to work; but the home is not an inn. Our personal customers (family members) are waiting there anxiously for us with good behaviour, pleasant smile, enthusiasm and full of happiness and with a lot of hope from us.

We, however, unaware of all this, reach home tired and half dead and dab their spirits and hopes. Whenever you go back home after office or the day's work, step in like a victor. Similarly, when you step out in the morning, say such words that the family spends a good day; not something that they spend the whole day sulking about. It is the purpose of every individual to keep his family happy and never forget this purpose.

Most of us slowly get so used to our wrong habits that we don't even get to know when we fall victim to it and by the time we get to realize it, it is already too late.

Hard Work/Toil

Hard work is the key to success; this is taught in every textbook in school. However, there is no dearth of such people who you will find saying that they did a lot of hard work but did not achieve anything. Is what we learnt in school and what is being taught even today, all wrong? I feel that we probably have a wrong idea of hard work. Hard work means such a positive and creative work which is not easy, is difficult and doing which may not be comfortable or easy.

On NDTV, there was a news that a social institution had commended such a couple who was generally a scavenger and had three sons. As we all know, the mentality of such families is that they take their children along with them so that they can earn more. However, this couple decided not to take their children in their profession. Instead they decided to educate them. Their neighbours used to laugh at this decision of theirs and would instigate them to take their children with them for at least 1-2 hrs, but they did not do so, because of which they had to work harder than the rest of them. However, the result of this was that their eldest son has passed class XII, the second son has passed class X and the youngest son has passed class VIII.

When we eat, we first use our mouths and the food later, goes into the stomach. We all know that the work is less in the mouth than in the stomach. This is the reason why some people eat more of junk food; because it tastes good; but it is bad for health.

But, in life, what happens is the opposite of this. We have to toil first and we get the taste later. In my opinion, in the long run, working and continuing to do so is hard work.

You will all agree that the toil of that couple is yielding results and will yield more fruit because their children have seen them toil and have learnt to labour.

All those who used to laugh at them, sigh today and wish that they had also done the same; then they would also be leading a better life with their families.

Now, you yourselves decide whether hard work yields success or not. 'Before you decide, definitely think; think a million times but not after taking a decision."

> ***"If you are courageous, listen to your heart, if you are a coward, then listen to your brain."***

Letter of a Father to His Son

W. Livingston Larned wrote such an 'immortal' letter to his son that hundreds of copies of that letter have been printed. It is presented here for you.

"Listen son! I am saying this to you. When you are in deep slumber, your small hand is under your cheek and the golden strands of your hair are sticking to your wet forehead. I alone have come stealthily into your room. A few minutes back when I was sitting in the library, reading the newspaper, a wave of regret ran inside me. Guiltily, I came near your bed.

Son, I was thinking about these things: I was angry with you; I scolded you while you were getting ready for school because you had just wet the towel and wiped your face. I reprimanded you for not cleaning my shoes. When you threw the things down on the floor, I screamed at you in anger.

At the breakfast table also I found fault with you. You dropped things, you swallowed your food without chewing it properly. You kept your elbows on the table. You put a lot of butter on the bread and when you started playing and I moved ahead to catch the train, you waved your hand towards me and said, 'Goodbye, dad!' I made a face and replied, 'Do not push your shoulders forward.'"

□

The Small Boy, Who is Walking behind me...

I want to walk very carefully,
Because a small boy is walking behind me;
I cannot take the risk of wandering,
Because I fear that he will also go astray.
I cannot escape his sight even once.
Whatever he sees me do, he also does.
He says that he will also be like me,
That small boy who is walking behind me.
While walking I must remember
That between the summer sun and
the snow of the cold,
I am creating for years—
That small child, who is walking behind me

Source: The Winning Attitude
Writer: John C.

G — Go
O — on
D — Duty

R — Return
O — On
T — Time
I — Invested

11

Love Your Work

Assessment of Oneself

Once a small child, whose age must be about 10-12 years, went to a general store. There, he asked the shopkeeper for permission to make a phone call. The shopkeeper pointed out the public phone to him. Because the child was short in height, he took the help of a stool lying nearby. He climbed on the stool and made his phone call. When he got through, he said, "Madam, I have seen your lawn and feel that you need a gardener. Madam, I need a job desperately. Can you give me employment?" The reply from the other end was, "There is a boy already working for me. Hence, I do not need any one else."

The boy again said, "Madam, I am very hard working. I will put my heart and soul into the work and will not take any leave." The reply from the other end was, "The boy who works for me has all these qualities. Hence, I do not require you." The boy, once again, said, "Madam, I am willing to work for even half the salary that you are paying that boy." The reply from the other end was, "Even if you were willing to work for free, yet, I would not change my gardener because I am fully satisfied with his work." The child put down the phone quietly. The shopkeeper was listening to his conversation with a lot of attention. He felt pity for him and so he said, "Son, I heard your conversation. If you want, I can give you work in my garden."

The child said, "Thank you, Sir, but I already have a job." Surprised, the shopkeeper asked, "Then are you looking for a second job." The child said, "No, Sir. I was ringing up my employer only under a changed name, only to find out if she was happy with my work or not. I am satisfied that she is happy with my work and that she is not willing to employ anyone else even if he is willing to work for free." So saying, the child went away from there. Seeing the love the child had towards his work, the shopkeeper got tears in his eyes. In his heart, he started thinking, "Oh! That everyone in our country became so honest towards his work, then how much progress our country would make."

From my experience of the seminars till now, I have found that generally people have a general complaint against their company that their salaries are little meaning that the company gives them less salary. This frustration is clearly visible in their way of working and in the way they behave with their colleagues. Usually, such people are always unhappy, keep complaining, try to incite others and come to work only to mark their attendance. They do not work with their hearts in it and do only as much work as is necessary to keep their jobs safe. Such people take more interest in strikes, etc.

People should try to make themselves deserving, not demanding. If an individual is deserving, then he does not need to demand and if he is not deserving, then he will not get anything even if he demands it, and if he gets it for some time, then he will get into the habit of living his life by demanding things.

I advise people to evaluate and ask them that if they leave their service with the company, then the amount of salary you will be paid outside in some other company is actually your market value. If your price is more, then you are working at little salary and your condition is justified and if it is not so, then be grateful to the company and try, continuously, to make yourself deserving.

Become Deserving; not Demanding

At seminars, one question that is asked very often is, "If a person shirks work and talks of random things and wastes his and his colleagues' and the company's time, but because of his cunningness, is never caught; he continues to get the same salary and the same conveniences as those who are hard working, then what effect will it have on us. Is it not natural for our morale to go down?"

It is my belief that a person who does not do any work but takes a salary is not an employee but a 'thief or a beggar'. He is not deserving of the salary even though the company is paying it to him. Whatever may be the reason for the company tolerating him, in the coming time, he will definitely stumble in life; because neither is he in the habit of working hard nor will he be able to inculcate it in his children. This will result in worthless children and a dark future!

Whether anyone else sees it or not, you yourself and God are always watching your activities. I don't think that any self-respecting man would like his child to be reared or brought up on income earned from thievery or begging. Hence, it is essential that when we are at work, then we must earn our salary so that we feel proud when we take it home! And we are able to say that it is not the company but 'I', who am raising my family! Make your enthusiasm your nature. If we enjoy our work then at least three-fourths of our life will be joyous. But how many such people do you find, in your life, who are satisfied with their work?

Another reason for the dissatisfaction at work is not salary, but the lack of enthusiasm. Nothing is interesting if you are not interested. If we can make our uninteresting work interesting, then we will enjoy doing it too. In the words of Swami Vivekanand, "If we get the work that we like, then even a foolish person can complete it. An intelligent person is one who can make every work interesting." If every second, we feel that the last ball of the match still remains and that for victory, we need to score only two runs, then that fervour will change us from ordinary to extraordinary.

Just as the difference of only a degree changes water into steam and steam can drive engines, similarly enthusiasm also works for our lives. In the words of Saint Thiruvalluvar, "Enthusiasm is the touchstone of an individual's fortune."

Another reason for not enjoying one's work or not wanting to do a certain work, is lack of patience. It is the result of this only that some people's mind keeps wandering from one work to the other. "The musk is within the deer but he searches for it in the forest."

Enthusiasm is Like Magnet

It does not matter how knowledgeable or brilliant you are. If you do not have a feeling of submission, then there is no use of your brilliance either. Similarly, if you are not very brilliant, but have enthusiasm, then everything is possible for you. Even if you do not expect any cooperation from other people, seeing your efforts, they will start giving you their mute support. The more enthusiastic you continue to remain about your work, the more positive will be the effect on the people around you and you will be able to achieve your goals faster with their help. Just as a magnet attracts the iron close to it, similarly enthusiasm also attracts others and also makes your environment enthusiastic.

In the entire history, there have been only two classes of people; one who earns wealth and the other who spends it.

Discipline is Beneficial

Work makes us get into the habit of working, habit makes character and character makes destiny. Instead of being lazy and waiting for an opportunity to strike, make it a habit to do hard work every day. Irrigate the tree of destiny with sweat and see it grow and blossom. Fate favours only those who make the effort and do not accept defeat. For them, even an impossible work becomes possible. Know what you desire, believe what you know, work with your heart in it, all the treasures of the earth will open up for you.

I held seminars at the plant of a company for 18 days continuously. The company wanted to cover all the employees of that plant in one month only. Under such a circumstance, I had to conduct one day's seminar for various batches continuously for 18 days.

On the 5th day, during lunch, their VP-HR asked me, "Sureshji, I have been watching you for the past four days. You are using the slides and telling incidents the same way and I know that you must be conducting at least 20 such seminars every month. Don't you feel bored saying the same thing every day?" I said to him, "Sir, ever since I have been born, I have been breathing. Till today, I have not felt bored. Everywhere I go in India, people respect me. I don't get bored. My bank balance keeps on increasing and I don't feel bored. So how can I get bored with something because of which I am getting so much?"

Has Amitabh Bachchan got bored of acting?

Have the Ambani brothers got bored of earning so much money?

Has Sachin stopped running for runs?

Has Lata Mangeshkar got bored of singing?

This is also a secret of the success of successful people—they do their usual work with more enthusiasm every day, yet they do not get bored of it.

Maintaining the Qualities is not just a Process, It is a Habit

You must be aware of 'Mitsushita Electronics' (National and now, Panasonic brand), a famous Japanese company. It made significant contributions in upholding the economy of Japan at one time and it was one of the selective and better companies of Japan. The name of the man who set up this company was Konosuke Mitsushita. There was a time when more than 2,50,000 people used to work in this company.

Konosuke Mitsushita had educational qualifications only up to class VI and he always used to remain unwell. He was physically a weak person but his willpower was equally strong.

Once a journalist asked Mitsushita to tell him the secret of his success. The reply Mitsushita gave was, "Every morning when I wake up, I see my own reflection in the mirror and repeat one sentence and that is 'My best performance is not the best'. This means that I shall have to bring about more improvement in myself and also my company."

Now, you think for yourselves that the producer of such a large company is saying every day that his best performance is also not the best. It requires more improvement while on the other hand some of us consider ourselves the best and feel that any suggestion to improve ourselves is foolish. Such a psyche can ruin both—the direction and condition of our lives.

Hence, we must also inculcate and not reduce the habit of 'a little more hard work'. A common man pays only as much attention to work and works only as much as is necessary to safeguard his job or to remain in business. However, those people who make it a habit to work a little more along with this, only they reach the summit of success. It is for us to decide whether we want 'a little more' or 'a little less'.

Japanese Quality

Once an American company gave a Japanese company an order to manufacture one part. The condition of the order was that not more than ten parts out of 1,00,000 could be bad, not more.

The Japanese company fulfilled that order and sent 1,00,000 correct parts and 10 spoilt parts. Along with that they sent a letter in which it was written that "We had a little difficulty in understanding your order. That is why we have made ten faulty parts and are sending them along with the order."

Sometimes, quality is not the work that is done but a habit that stays in our minds day and night and used in our behaviour. Maintaining quality is also a habit and not maintaining quality is also a habit, but that is known as a 'bad' habit. It is because of this bad habit that one has to face difficulties in the times to come.

□

The customer forgets the price quickly, If he gets good quality.

Being together and working together are two different things.

12

Make a Winning Team

The team that wins is considered good. If there is no victory, such a team is not considered good. Hence, we should have the desire to make a winning team, not a team of victorious people. The best example of this is our Indian Cricket team wherein on an individual level, everyone is victorious (which means that all records are in their names) yet we lose most of the matches. Whereas, on the other hand is the Australian team wherein everyone of the team is individually, not a record holder, yet their team wins most of the matches. What we need to do is to get our team into the habit of winning.

The Japanese are well aware of this thing. They know the importance of success very well. Team work means working together at the centre of success in the world market.

"Kadam kadam badhaye ja, khushi ke geet gaye ja"—these are the first lines of the inspiring song of the Azaad Hind Fauj of Subhash Chandra Bose. However, this song is applicable to any company, even if it is a company of three or three thousand employees. Business is like any complicated machine. To work it, all the parts work together easily.

Need of the Hour—A Successful Team

To succeed, all members of the teams of any thinking must understand this and cooperate. For the creation of a musical piece, players of all the instruments have to play their instruments. Along with the full creation, they also have to pay attention to their own instrument. If all the players played different tunes, it would create a harsh sound. In a boat race, that team is the fastest, the members of which team row with coordination and full strength. Have you ever wondered at the selection of a certain player in the team? Probably, he is a brilliant player individually, but he is probably not willing to sacrifice his prestige for the welfare of his team.

As a leader, you need to determine that instead of brilliant workers, you have brilliant associates.

1. Feeling of Equal Sacrifice

Mr. Lei Iacocca used to take a salary of $1 instead of $ 10,00,000. If a leader sacrifices his today for tomorrow, then his supporters also will willingly and naturally follow him and the team will work in an influential way. Iacocca calls it 'the flowing of the same amount of blood'.

Do you work from 9 in the morning to 5 in the evening or do you work from 5 in the morning to 9 in the morning? If, for the sake of unity, you work for sixteen hours, then you can hope to make your employees work for more hours.

When you talk, your comrades listen and when you work, your comrades watch. Hence, you have to be cautious about whatever you do or make them do. Every action of yours has an effect on others. Therefore, try to be the ideal on issues of work. No other remedy is as effective and as intoxicating as a visible example. Similarly, if everyone is suffering the same amount of problems then it is definite that any goal can be achieved easily.

Whether it is work or the play field, every team is like a family, which, it is said, is like a chariot. All the employees in any business are like the parts, parcel and wheels of this family which is like a chariot. So that the chariot runs in a good way, it is essential that all parts function properly. If one wheel functions badly, the whole chariot can topple over. If any wheel starts running slowly, then the direction of the chariot will change and instead of going forward, it can turn backwards. If there is only one wheel, then, instead of moving forward, the chariot will keep rotating at one point only. The horses that pull the chariot also have to run at the same speed. This is what working together is. We must never forget the significance of equal sacrifice if we have to get the work done.

2. Mixing with Colleagues

This depends upon your attitude towards them. What you think about your colleagues and yourself.

If your thinking about yourself is not correct, then it will be difficult for you to think correctly about your colleagues and working with them. When someone does some good work, definitely take time out to praise them. Always be on the lookout for such occasions. Never forget to express your sentiments, thanks and smile at your colleagues. Keep golden words and a golden pen with you always. Praise your colleagues by patting their backs. You may rest assured that that praise will definitely reach them and you will become their favourite because of your good nature.

Only if you are honest towards your customers and your colleagues, can you expect honesty from your colleagues. Be honest and look honest too. Do you express your enthusiasm, initiative, allegiance and support towards your organization and its employees? If the answer is yes, then the employees will also reciprocate in the same manner. Do you really ask for their suggestions? And after some suggestions have been implemented, do you give them credit or a reward for it?

Remember, a positive attitude is not born out of high position or wealth. The truth is that a high position is secured only because of a positive attitude

This is as true as the statement that you do not smile because you are happy; you are happy because you smile. Be the master of a positive attitude.

3. Place Yourself in the Position of Others

Every member of the team has his or her own problems. Look at the problems from their point of view and try to solve their problems to the best of your ability. Even if the problem does not get solved, the feeling to make an effort to solve the problems has some meaning. Even the person who works with you will have the consolation that you, at least, made an effort to solve their problems. Placing yourself in others' position will inculcate better cooperation amongst the members of the team. Whether others do it or not, you must take the initiative to cooperate. Carry out selfless cooperation in line with your nature. Give the credit due to people who cooperate. Never take lightly the idea of cooperating with your colleagues. Tell him how his good habit is cooperating in achieving the ultimate aim of organization.

If the individual does not care about the credit, then there is no limit to his ability.

Create a special group around yourself. American billionaire and oil industrialist J. Paul Ghettos calls the members of such a group 'the people of a millionaire psyche'. These people are such supporters who are progressive in their thinking, who are conscious of the cost and are disposed towards profits and such supporters create a team around them. Later, this team becomes a pyramid to touch the moon.

You should become more responsible. If you do not give work to a person who does his share of work, then working together will turn out to be a failure. A team becomes stronger with propriety, haste and determination. Once you get to know the outlook of your colleague, it becomes easier to work. If not after the second, at least after the third warning, turn him out of the team. Spread the message of 'brighten up or quit'. After this you will see that each member is doing his share of work with all his strength.

Encourage the employees to learn new expertise to make themselves more useful for the team and continue to make the work more challenging. Keep changing the place of work of the players', that is, of the employees, not for a change but do this to make them aware of the correct place to play or work and of the problems of the member of his team.

4. Make the Correct Communication

Give the right importance to this. Expect that the boss gives the clear message, uses simple words and speaks in a peaceful manner like the Buddha. Do you do the same while working with the members of your team and how is your body language? Do you know how much you speak, how much you can say without using words? Do you know that in Japan, things unsaid are considered more important than what has been said?

5. Meaningful Conversation with Your Colleagues Works like 'Open Sim Sim'

Learn to listen with attention. Believe me, it is an extremely difficult work. We have never learnt to listen carefully. Remember the school and college days and you will understand that you have neither done any course in listening carefully nor have you read any book. This is probably the reason why in your childhood, your parents used to complain that you never listened to them. Now even your wife has the same complaint.

Nobody can tolerate the loss of not listening carefully to his colleague, yet he does not listen carefully. We have all grown up under this delusion that only talking is everything, not listening.

We are discussing meaningful talk with our colleagues. How can you talk to them without listening? Is this not the right thing? Along with saying what you have to say, also listen to them carefully too.

Come to the level of a colleague and listen: It is very difficult to do this, but with incessant efforts, you will slowly learn. This way, you will be able to learn of their desire and their assent. Go down to their level. High status is not beneficial for information.

Buddhism

There was a Buddist mendicant. He was a very good hermit. There have been only a handful of hermits in this world. He was one of them. If you went to meet him, he would always sit with his back turned towards you, facing the wall. People used to get very offended by this act of his and asked, "What kind of etiquette is this? We have come to meet you and you are sitting with your face towards the wall and your back towards us."

The Buddhist mendicant used to say, "When one faces the wall, at least one thing always stays in the mind—it is a wall. If it does not listen there is no harm it is a wall. But, if I face you, there will be a lot of harm. We continue talking but you don't listen. You are also like the wall. So that I do not lose my temper, I keep facing the wall. There is no need to get angry with the wall. A wall is a wall, after all. If it does not listen, there is no harm. But you are a human being. You also do not listen. That is why I have my back towards you."

You will have to inspire your colleagues to be. Tell them not only to give you the facts but also well thought out suggestions.

Learn to write: Remember, with practice, you can become better and some day, become the best completely. Instead of talking, you can convey what you want to say in a better way by writing.

There are many ways to convey the correct and clear message by writing. Organize your thoughts before writing them. First create an ordinary sketch in your mind and then on paper. Think over it while sleeping and being awake. Keep making the corrections. Then start to write. You will see that thoughts flow out like water from a fountain. Keep making sketches one after the other. Do not forget to keep a smile on your face while you write. Do you know what will happen with this? Your smile will reflect in your writing. Do not think! Just start off.

Write the important things on a paper. Do not make 'the best' an enemy of 'better'. Express your thoughts in a short and clear way. Remember thoughts are read, not as a novel but as a letter. For the main things, use stars and dots. Write what you want to say, clearly. Take the opinion of others after writing. Remember, your job is not to boast but to acquire suggestions and directions.

Use Your Own Style

This is your letter. Hence, speak in your own style. Paragraph is an independent unit of thought. Therefore, use paragraphs. These must be in the proper sequence. Use words that are used in common spoken language. Then, later, edit them. Remember, spoken words are temporary, while written words are permanent. Written words are like a double-edged sword, hence, a lot of care is required in their usage. Do not delay. Later on, you will have to suffer a lot of monetary loss. What will you do if your brain stops functioning? Maintain contact with such people who can freely give you advice. Many people feel very happy when asked for advice.

6. Give Your Colleagues the Work of their Choice

If they do not get any challenging work, then the colleagues lose the enthusiasm. Some one has said a very intelligent thing; if you choose the work of your choice, then you will not need to work even one day.

You only are responsible for your colleague's interesting or boring work. The work must be self-satisfactory. This brings out the brilliance of your colleague to the forefront. Work is not just a means to earn money. It must be an act through which we can develop.

In order to reduce this shortcoming, give your colleagues jobs that they do not want but which they desire—is this not an impractical thing? It probably is. But a good organizer tries to change impractical thoughts into reality as far as he can. It is a challenge for them and they enjoy facing such challenges.

One should utilize a colleague's skill of knowledge. Only assurance will not work. See to it that your colleague gets so much satisfaction from his work that he is completely dedicated to it. Those who try, even if it is for the proverbial nth time, will definitely succeed. If you tell a lie or give help, then an average colleague also tries so much that the work becomes comparatively more challenging and he throws all that he had vowed into it.

How does one find out about a colleague who is involved in an inappropriate place?

- He will seem totally lost and will show as if he is not present there.
- His eyes will not have the spark in them, he will walk slowly and will become cranky.

How can you improve such a condition? There is probably no one single or permanent solution for this.

Such a situation cannot be improved in one day or one month. You will have to continue trying. Give your colleague new work and new responsibility. Till such time that he gets the proper work, keep giving him different kinds of work. Yes, this is the only solution. To find out which work your colleague likes and which he does not like, analyse it and keep an eye on him. Generally, some colleague does some work with a lot of enthusiasm but after sometime, becomes indifferent towards it. This is because of duplication or boredom or may be someone has hurt his ego with some sarcastic remark. Try to find out and be patient. Once you come to know the signs and the problem, you can talk to him and ultimately, hoping for betterment, you will find out the necessary solution. Successful managers do this work on a regular basis and slowly, they become experts in finding out interesting work for their colleagues.

7. Hand Over Work but do not Forget

80% of the work that comes to your table can be settled immediately. Your competence is hidden in handing over the work to the most worthy colleague. This is no laughing matter because generally you want to do the work meant for you, yourself. Many of us consider it convenient to do the work ourselves rather than managing the work. An impressive manager does not forget the work that he has deputed someone else to do.

How can one acquire this competence? It is very easy but for this it is essential that

- Subsequent list—who has to be given which job—note this down in a list
- Investigating list—This list is made for determining the daily, weekly, fortnightly and monthly progress.

It is a very easy and common work to make both these lists but majority of the managers does not prepare this list. Handing over a work is considered to be an art. You can learn this art with your knowledge and experience and take it in your behaviour.

While deputing work, pay special attention to its purpose, importance and the time allotted to complete the work. Do not think that your colleague knows everything or that he will ask you something about it. Know that he will not ask you anything. He will give priority to the work in accordance with his understanding and necessity.

- After deputing the work ask your colleague what you have told him? This will be a very good thing; because this way you will get an idea what and how much of what you have told him, he has understood.
- Create a spirit of challenge in your colleague while handing over a job to him.
- Ascertain progress on the work from time to time and offer assistance, but do not give your consent beyond limit.

- Do not expect that if you had done the work yourself, you would have done it better. Review the work. Accept the result and praise the good work. After all this, like a father, let him know with love, how the work could have been done better.

□

**Continue, Continue,
Continue with Perseverance.**

13

A Winner Never Gets Tired and One Who Gets Tired Never Wins

Lord Buddha

Once Lord Buddha was going somewhere. On the way he saw that many pits had been dug up. He longed to know the reason for this. He asked a local farmer, "Who has dug these pits and for what purpose?" That old farmer said, "In search of water, a passerby tried to dig these holes. He would dig a few feet deep and not finding water there he would start digging another hole. But he did not get the water." Lord Buddha said, "That man lacked patience. Had he dug the first hole deeper, with patience, he would definitely have found water. A mixture of labour and patience, always brings success."

Edison's Laboratory

Edison was carrying out an experiment in his laboratory. He had taken on a young scientist as an apprentice. That young scientist was very thoughtful, argumentative and brilliant. He would be involved

18 hours a day with his experiments and every night would return home unsuccessful. After three months, the apprentice gave up. He would have given up a long time back, but seeing the flame of faith in the eyes of Edison, he could not build up the courage to say anything to him. Every morning, at the break of day, Edison would run to his laboratory like an inquisitive child. The youth, on the other hand, would come every day with the determination that he would say, "Forgive me, but this work is beyond our ability. This experiment will never be successful. We have probably taken a wrong experiment in hand. So many times we have done so many experiments in so many directions and each time in the end, all we get is defeat, yet, like mad people, we continue working on it. Leave this. Let us do something which will bring us success." However, seeing the burning fire in Edison's eyes, he did not have the courage to say it. He felt that it was not right that Edison who was old, behaved young and he, although young, should talk like an old man. Yet three months passed. There was no peace during the day and no sleep at night.

One morning, after three months, he did not look Edison in the eye. With his eyes on the ground, he said to Edison, "Please forgive me." Edison said, "Look into my eyes and say it." He said, "The moment I raise my eyes I get perplexed. For the last three months, I have been talking with my eyes raised continuously, but today, I have no intention of raising my eyes. This experiment is not going to be successful." Edison said, "Have you gone mad or what? After coming so close to success!" The youth said, "Close to success? You are not even as close as you were on the first day. All the experiments that you did for three months, all turned out to be useless."

Edison said, "You don't know Mathematics. We have seen so many ways, they have all been useless. This means that now the number of useless ways has reduced. We have seen two hundred paths. If there had been three hundred paths, now, only one hundred paths are left. We are coming close to success. If not today, then tomorrow; if not tomorrow, then the day after tomorrow—we will surely succeed. One way, at least, would be right; one that will take us close to success! And you are losing. After three months of toil, you are thinking of returning whereas the goal of success is shining just before you.

This is what devotion is. Devotion means the belief of victory in the face of defeat! Devotion is the formula of victory and success in the face of defeat and success. A stone on the path can be considered a hindrance or a stepping stone to success. If you consider it a hindrance, then the journey of victory will end there only and if you consider it the stepping stone to success, then the journey to victory will go further ahead. Situation is the same, but how we perceive it is different and this difference can be removed with devotion.

The Punishment to Eat Onions

Once, while punishing a thief, the king said, "We give you the opportunity to select your punishment.

Tell us, would you like the punishment of eating a hundred onions or a hundred lashings or would you rather pay a fine of ₹ 1000? Of these three, which one is acceptable to you?" The thief thought, instead of paying a thousand rupees or taking a thousand lashings, it is better to eat the onions. He selected eating onions but he was in a bad condition after eating only 15 onions. He said to the king, "My Lord, I shall take a hundred lashings only." However, he had taken only 25 lashings, when his skin tore and he started bleeding and it started paining badly. Once again, he pleaded to the king that he would eat the onions only, but after eating only 50 onions, he changed his decision once again and requested for lashings. It continued this way only till he had not taken 80 onions and 90 lashings!

□

Success cannot be got cheap;
however, it is never expensive.

It is generally the lazy and the irresponsible people who weep about destiny.

14

Fortune

Generally, at conferences, I am asked questions about 'Fortune' and if there is anything by the name of 'Fortune'? and, what is its contribution in our success or failure? Although this question is very common, yet I could never understand the correct answer to this. However, on the basis of my experience and information till now, it is my belief that 'Fortune is nothing but the union of opportunity and preparation.'

We generally see that we do not prepare ourselves to receive success meaning that we are not excited about receiving success and instead of concentrating on essential and necessary work; we pay more attention to unimportant and unnecessary work. This is the reason why we either miss the opportunities or do not make proper use of them. It is these kinds of people who are perpetually crying over their misfortune.

It is true that everything in our life does not happen according to our desire, but we must continue doing whatever is within the bounds of our authority, with effort and preparation. It is my belief that God is neither blind, nor deaf; He definitely gives us fruit for the true labour we do.

Therefore, we need to get on with our work with perseverance and always be aware so that we can find the right opportunities and achieve success. "If you get the opportunity, good; otherwise keep searching for the opportunity." Someone has rightly said, "God helps those who help themselves", meaning even God helps those who are strong. There are some people who, after finding the seeds of the good fruit, put it in their pockets and go around in the hope that a tree will sprout out of the seed and one day, they will get the fruit too; because a seed leads to a tree and a fruit is born to a tree. Hence, preparation means developing our qualities and keeping our mentality positive and creative so that the seed of opportunity can be sown in it. We will be able to get a tree from the seed and fruit from the tree only when we sow the seed in the correct and fertile soil and irrigate it with water, sunshine and manure. Similarly, when we irrigate the seed of opportunity with the manure of hard work and determination, then we definitely get the fruit of success.

However, some people lack patience. They throw the seeds on the ground but they keep pulling it out from the ground every day to look at it. It is for such people that bit has been said that if you put the seed in the ground and water it and take it out the next day to see it, then all they will get is 'wet seeds'. In the same way, the seed of opportunity needs, besides hard work and determination, the sunlight of patience too.

The Story of the Black Bamboo

The seed of the black bamboo appears to be like a dry fruit with a very hard shell. After sowing this seed, practically every week, it needs to be given manure and irrigated. An amateur harvester gets very depressed on seeing that nothing happens the first year. It is given manure and water the second year round too, yet it does not show any result. The process of giving it manure and irrigating, it is repeated in the third and the fourth year also, yet nothing is visible. Then, in the sixth month of the fifth year, it sprouts and within the sixth week, the bamboo grows 40 feet. Now, the question that comes up is, did the bamboo grow 40 feet in six weeks or in five years? What do you think? It is our belief that this growth is the result of all the incidents that occurred during the last few years because if the process of manure and water had been stopped during this period, then the seed would have died as a seed itself.

There is a disease that occurs only amongst human beings. It is called 'Paralysis of Analysis'. Such people never say yes for any new work and basing it on some kind of statistics, keep discouraging others too. They are probably not aware that history also has its limits as in it gives information only about what has happened. History cannot tell us what could have been done or what could have happened. You will generally find such people saying, "Oh! Has such a thing ever happened?" or "Have you ever heard such a thing happen?" or "We have spent all our lives but have never seen or heard such a thing" or "I can give it in writing that such a thing has never happened nor can it ever happen."

L	—	***Labour***
U	—	***Under***
C	—	***Correct***
K	—	***Knowledge***

□□□